Cook

Pardoner

Monk

Doctor

Wife of Bath

CHAUCER IN HIS TIME

Chaucer reading to the Court

Chaucer

IN HIS TIME

DEREK BREWER

THOMAS NELSON AND SONS LTD
LONDON

THOMAS NELSON AND SONS LTD
Parkside Works Edinburgh 9
36 Park Street London W1
117 Latrobe Street Melbourne C1

THOMAS NELSON AND SONS (AFRICA) (Pty) LTD
P.O. Box 9881 Johannesburg

THOMAS NELSON AND SONS (CANADA) LTD
91-93 Wellington Street West   Toronto 1

THOMAS NELSON AND SONS
18 East 41st Street New York 17, N.Y.

SOCIÉTÉ FRANÇAISE D'ÉDITIONS NELSON
97 rue Monge Paris 5

———

Printed in Great Britain by
Thomas Nelson (Printers) Ltd London and Edinburgh

CONTENTS

ILLUSTRATIONS

PREFACE

THE present book attempts to give an account of how life looked and felt round about Chaucer; it is to that extent a sketch of the general culture of his times. Chaucer's life and works have been used to give focus, but they are not directly discussed, and it is not necessary to know anything about them, or about the period in general, to understand this book: though I hope that a reading of this book will help the understanding and enjoyment of Chaucer's poetry, and also of a fascinating historical period.

After the introductory chapters, which set the scene and introduce most of the main 'characters', the book follows roughly the course of a man's life in the late fourteenth century. The emphasis is mainly on the court because that was the chief centre of high culture, and the centre of most of Chaucer's activities. Inevitably there has been less said about, for example, the life of the poor, or about such non-courtly activities as the miracle plays or monasticism, which were outside my brief.

It is not the plan, in this series, to give detailed references for all the statements made, but I must express my debt to the chief modern authorities, to whom any reader must turn if he wishes to go further into the subject. I have made much use of Professor McKisack's *The Fourteenth Century*, The Clarendon Press, Oxford, 1959, which has very full references. I am also indebted to Edith Rickert, *Chaucer's World*, edited by C. C. Olson and M. M. Crow, The Clarendon Press, Oxford, 1948; and to H. B. Workman, *John Wycliffe*, The Clarendon Press, Oxford, 1926. Quotations from *Piers Plowman*, *Sir Gawain and the Green Knight*, and other poems, though I have modernized them, have been based on texts published by The Early English Text Society. Quotations from Chaucer have been taken from *The Complete Works of Chaucer*, edited by F. N. Robinson, 2nd edition, O.U.P., London, 1957, (copyright Houghton Mifflin & Co., Boston), with marginal glosses added where they seem necessary for those unfamiliar with Chaucer's language. Quotations from Froissart are all taken from *The Chronicles of England, France and Spain*, translated by Thomas Johnes, H. G. Bohn, London, 1852.

It also gives me pleasure to acknowledge the help received in various conversations with my friends and colleagues R. H. Hilton, P. Sawyer, G. T. Shepherd. A lecture by Mr K. B. MacFarlane, of Magdalen College, Oxford, suggested to me a new way of regarding the Lollard Knights. The responsibility for any opinions expressed and any mistakes I have made is of course entirely my own.

The illustrations have been chosen as far as possible from known English work of the period, though there are one or two exceptions. They have been chosen not primarily for their beauty but to illustrate and extend the references in the text. I should like to acknowledge the help of Miss Dawn Maguire in obtaining them.

Grateful thanks are also due to the following for permission to quote copyright material:
The Royal Historical Society for quotations from *The Sermons of Thomas Brinton, Bishop of Rochester*, edited by Sister Mary Aquinas Devlin, 1954 (Camden, Third Series, Vol. 85); Manchester University Press for quotations from *The Anonimalle Chronicle*, edited by V. H. Galbraith; The Clarendon Press for quotations from *The English Landscape, Medieval England*, by W. G. Hoskins, edited by A. L. Poole, and Chandos Herald: *Life of the Black Prince*, edited and translated by M. R. Pope and E. C. Lodge.

D. S. BREWER

If one can really penetrate the life of another age, one is penetrating the life of one's own.

T. S. ELIOT

CHAPTER ONE

Merry England

THE English Middle Ages were once thought of as bright gay times, when, except for a few patches of discontent, people were satisfied with their various positions in life, wore bright clothes, worked at healthy jobs, danced round the maypole in May, and clustered in winter round a cheerful log fire, listening to the local storyteller or the wandering minstrel. Churches were painted even on the outside, and inside jewels and frescoes glowed in the dim religious light; palaces were gloriously decked, but not more so than their happy inmates; there were colourful processions on frequent holidays, through neat towns gay with gardens and orchards. The tournament was the bright equivalent of the Saturday afternoon sport of a drab industrial society. Knights were brave and courteous, ladies beautiful, gracious, and chaste; tradesmen cheerful and prosperous; peasants sturdy, independent and faithful. There is much truth in this picture. Medieval writers and painters of manuscripts were the first to feel the glamour of the Middle Ages, the glamour of the times in which they themselves lived. The man who felt it most was the Flemish writer Froissart, whose Chronicles, written in French, are not only an important historical source-book, but have been the delighted reading of six European centuries. Chaucer himself felt this same delight in his time and rendered it in such poems as *The Knight's Tale*. Are we so conscious of the delight and glamour of being alive in our own times?

Yet it is also easy to paint a totally different picture of the Middle Ages, and this has been characteristically the task of some recent writers. From their point of view one hardly knows whether to be more appalled by the wickedness or the stupidity of men in the Middle Ages; by their sufferings or their cruelty; their ignorance or their crass inefficiency; their filth, or the dreariness of most of their clothing and their lives. The motives of men of those times are interpreted in terms of the lowest selfishness, greed, prejudice, and

Froissart presents his book to Richard II

inhumanity. The very word *medieval* has become in popular journalism a word of abuse—very often applied to what is characteristic of later times, like the witchcraft of the Renaissance, or the slums and *laissez-faire* capitalism of industrial England. Although men in the Middle Ages did not know the word *medieval* (their times were 'modern' to them, as we sometimes forget) they were also the first critics of the badness of their times. In the late fourteenth century the preachers called the tournament of the rich the torment of the poor. Cruelty, corruption, inefficiency, inequality were heartily condemned. Chaucer gives us plenty of examples.

We cannot help praising some things and blaming others, but simple views are not much use. Whatever the anxieties or difficulties of life in modern Europe or America, we are bound to see that enormous improvements have been made in the physical conditions of life since the fourteenth century. Yet that century is a time well worth knowing, for its intrinsic fascination, and for the way it enlarges our whole view of what it is to be English, of what it is to be human. There is no better way of looking at an historical period than through the literature of the time. It is of course only one way of looking, and by no means the only valuable way. One can approach the times in as many ways as there are subjects of study, through economic, political, ecclesiastical or military history, through the study of institutions, or of individual lives. I shall touch on these. But chiefly I shall try to suggest what life looked like as it went on round about Chaucer, the greatest poet of the century, and one of the three or four greatest English poets.[1]

The time is roughly the second half of the fourteenth century, for Chaucer was born about 1340-45 and died in 1400. It was a time of unusual restlessness and strain in war and wealth, in politics and social relations, in learning, and even in health, for the greatest plague disaster of all, the Black Death, occurred in 1348-9. Yet men still called England 'merry'. The first writer to do so, Henry of Huntingdon, had done so before 1150, writing in Latin of *Anglia plena jocis*. It is characteristically in the fourteenth century that the phrase is first used in English, by the anonymous author of the northern poem *Cursor Mundi*, who probably wrote early in the cen-

---

[1] For an account of Chaucer's life and discussion of his poetry, from a literary point of view, together with a short bibliography, see my *Chaucer*, second (revised) edition, Longmans, Green & Co. Ltd., 1961.

tury. Here the word 'merry' may mean 'pleasant', but it also began to mean 'cheerful, jolly' in the fourteenth century, and probably has a flavour of this meaning when applied to England. For see what the thirteenth-century encyclopaedist, the Franciscan Friar Bartholomew the Englishman, wrote about England. He wrote in Latin, but I quote a modernised form of the translation made in the late fourteenth century by Trevisa.

> England is a strong land and a sturdy, and the plenteousest corner of the world; so rich a land that scarcely it needeth help of any land, and every other land needeth help of England. England is full of mirth and of game, and men oft-times able to mirth and game; free men of heart and with tongue, but the heart is more better and more free than the tongue.

It was very rare for people to write about England, country or town, but when they did they described its pleasant fruitfulness. The West Midland author of *Mum and the Sothsegger*, writing about 1400, describes how he climbed to the top of a hill somewhere in the West Midlands and looked around

Beholding hedges and holts so green,
The mansions, and meadows mown all new,
For such was the season of the same year.
I lifted up my eyelids and looked further
And saw many sweet sights, so me God help,
The woods and waters and the well-springs
And trees trailed from top to the earth,
Curiously covered with kirtel of green,
The flowers in fields flavouring sweet,
The corn in the crofts cropped full fair,
The running river rushing fast,
Full of fish and of fry of manifold kind,
The briars with their berries bent over the ways,
As honeysuckles hanging on each half,
Chestnuts and cherries that children desire

4

Were lodged under leaves full lusty to see.
The hawthorn so wholesome I beheld also,
And how the beans bloomed, and the broom-flowers;
Pears and plums and peascods green,
That ladies lusty much look after.

He goes on to say that he saw many other fruits including grapes
(wine was made in the Vale of Evesham until the end of the fifteenth
century—perhaps the weather was milder?), and then how he saw
hounds chasing rabbits and hares, and how he saw sheep and lambs,
cows and horses, and hundreds of deer. The birds sang in every
hedge and their song, the sweet smells and the fresh sights, made all
his troubles vanish from him. Again, the note of praise is rare, to
say the least, in Wycliffe, but this is how he wrote of Oxford near
the end of his life:

> Not unworthily is it called the vineyard of the Lord. It was founded
> by the holy fathers and situated in a splendid site, watered by rills and
> fountains, surrounded by meadows, pastures, plains and glades. The
> mountains and hills around it ward off the spirit of the storm, while it
> is near to flourishing groves and leafy villages. I will sum up all in one
> word. Oxford is a place gladsome and fertile, so suitable for the habi-
> tation of the gods that it has been rightly called the house of God and
> the gateway of heaven.

Admittedly this is written up as a prelude to a terrific blast against
the friars who besmirch Oxford with their presence, but all three
passages show the kind of delightful, rich, well-cultivated landscape
that England could offer then, and the pleasure and pride Englishmen could take in it. Chaucer was too much a Londoner, too little
a countryman, too much a courtier and a reader, too little a sports-
man, to have much of this feeling. His landscapes are mostly French
literary landscapes, where May is kinder than it usually is in England.
All that his poetry tells us is that he had a little garden where once
he slept out at night, and fell asleep—'within an hour or two'.

It is easy to see why people loved a rich well-tilled landscape, and in literature wished for the most part to read of gardens, orchards, flowery meadows and sunny skies. The population in the second half of the century may have been as little as two and a quarter million; it was certainly no more than four million, and not likely to have been so large. Perhaps a third of the total area was 'waste'—mountains (and 'horrid' they must have appeared to a generation that could call, like Wycliffe, the mild protuberances round Oxford 'mountains'), moorlands, marsh and, above all, woodlands. Moreover, what is termed the 'colonisation' of the English landscape had reached its peak about 1300:

> ... behind this abstraction there lies a daily, blinding sweat, bloody at times, and backbreaking toil with axe and spade and saw. It was a slow world, a hand-made world, created yard by yard, at times almost inch by inch, by the labour of countless human beings out of the primordial chaos of timber, rock and water.[1]

After the Black Death of 1348-9 nature was slowly forcing men back in their hard battle, especially from the frontiers on the poorer lands. Houses fell first vacant then into ruin, even in well-established towns, where in the second half of the century there were plenty of waste open spaces like bombed sites after the war. No one wanted to 'get away from it all' for recreation; unworked nature was dangerous, and it is no wonder that the most loved landscape was the one made precious by human toil, where life itself could become more precious.

The most heavily populated and richest parts of the country were the south-eastern and eastern counties, with rich soil and easy communications, though no part of the country, except for the worst of mountain, moor and fen, was quite uninhabited, or really difficult to get at. Easy communications go far to account for the

[1] W. G. Hoskins, 'The English Landscape', *Medieval England*, ed. by A. L. Poole, The Clarendon Press, Oxford, 1958, p. 10.

early unity and harmony of England compared with her neighbours. 'Every mile or so in Eastern England one would have seen spires and towers rising from the fields, and fields populous with men, women and children tending the strips.'[1]

More than half the population consisted of serfs, i.e. villeins or bondmen, who were the lowest rank of society, and for whom the essence of their situation was that they were supposed to be bound to the land and to their lord's service. They could not move about or change their jobs just as they wanted to. They were not slaves, for they had certain legal rights, usually enshrined in 'the custom of the manor', but they were in some sense the property of whoever owned the estate, whether a secular lord or a monastery. They were bound to give labour services at special times, for example at harvest, before they worked on their own fields. They had to make all kinds of payments for food, fuel, or permission to do certain things; for instance, if a serf sold a cow he had to pay a proportion of the profit to the lord, and if he married his daughter to someone he had to pay a tax. When he died the estate owner was entitled to his best cow. Above all, he was not allowed to move from the estate, except with the lord's permission. At most times, however, men have preferred city lights to country airs, and London to other cities, and the fourteenth century was no exception.

There was no serfdom in cities. If a serf could run away and remain uncaptured in a city for a year he was free. Employers in the city were glad of his labour, and not inclined to question too closely his origins. Sometimes a serf was allowed to remain away if he paid his lord an annual fine. In the labour shortage that was particularly acute after the Black Death many a serf ran away to better-paid service and greater freedom in the towns, especially in London. Furthermore, some counties, like Kent, had very few serfs bound to the land, and when men are free they wander. Therefore

[1] Hoskins, op. cit., p. 27.

men came to London from all over England. It was as well they did. Medieval towns were so unhealthy that they could not possibly have kept up their numbers without a constant inflow from the country. Not only the lower classes sought their fortunes in the towns and in London. Chaucer refers to the crowd of clerics looking for easier or more interesting or better-paid jobs when he says of his own poor Parson, who had such a daily beauty in his life, that

> He sette nat his benefice to hyre
> And leet his sheep encombred in the myre   *left*
> And ran to Londoun unto Seinte Poules
> To seken hym a chaunterie for soules,   *chantry*
> Or with a bretherhed to been withholde ...   *gild; retained*
> > *General Prologue, The Canterbury Tales* I, ll. 507-11

Langland, Chaucer's contemporary, says,

> Parsons and parish priests complained to the bishop
> That their parishes were poor since the pestilence time,
> To have licence and leave in London to dwell,
> And sing there for simony, for silver is sweet.
> > *Piers Plowman*, C text (modernised) I, ll. 81-4

It was not in every case a bad thing. Some such 'clerks' were vital to the country's administration, such as it was. Perhaps the greatest of them was William Wykeham, Bishop of Winchester and Chancellor of England, founder of Winchester School and New College, Oxford, son of a serf in Lincolnshire.

The way in which London sucked in, then as now, men of every class and interest, is also illustrated by the alderman, Simon de Paris, who, notwithstanding his name, came of a family of Norfolk serfs, as well as by the two poets just quoted. Little is known about Langland, but it seems he came of a humble family somewhere about Malvern. His friends helped pay for some education, possibly a year or two at the university, and he took minor orders in the Church, though he never became a priest. Then he went to London, lived in the

London Bridge and the Tower

very disreputable quarter of Cornhill and made a poor living with
Kit his wife and Calotte his daughter, possibly as a professional
bedesman, praying for people's souls for payment. Chaucer's family
was much better off. His grandfather, Robert, owned property in
Ipswich, and was a vintner. He went into the King's service in the
wine customs (wine being by far England's greatest import) and
married a woman of a prosperous Ipswich family. His son John,
the poet's father, inherited the Ipswich property, and his father's
business, and became associated with the customs. He too moved

An artist's impression (from the Luttrell Psalter) of a medieval walled city, with church, inns (shown by bushes on poles), stone and timber houses, etc.

to London, and then became an important person in the general affairs of the city. He had a house in Lower Thames Street, which even today follows roughly the course it had in the fourteenth century (though the buildings are now no doubt much less picturesque), and it may have been in this house that Chaucer was born.

London was unique among English cities, being the centre of commercial power, with a special relationship to the king. It was near the main seat of the royal power, which was the city of Westminster, and was the biggest of English cities with a population of about 35,000. (Estimates for other towns are: York, about 11,000; Bristol, about 10,000; Plymouth and Coventry, about 7,000; no other town is thought to have had above 6,000; by contrast, contemporary Florence, one of the biggest cities in Europe, had about 90,000.) For all the slums, abuses, smells, and other disadvantages of a capital city, it seems to have been a pleasant place. The city was chiefly confined within the walls of the present mile-square City of London, abutting on the river. There were suburbs outside the walls, like Southwark, just over the river. Here began the Dover

Road, and the Pilgrims' Way to Canterbury. In Southwark was the Tabard Inn, at which Chaucer's pilgrims gathered, and the church (now the Cathedral) where the effigy of the poet John Gower, a friend of Chaucer, can still be seen. The road from London to the palace of Westminster went along the Strand, that is, along the river-bank, on which nobles had their town houses. The most famous of these was the Savoy, John of Gaunt's wonderful palace, built by his father-in-law Henry, Duke of Lancaster, crowded with beautiful treasures, and totally destroyed in the Revolt of 1381. The houses faced the road, and had long gardens running down to the river. St Martin's, then, was truly 'in the fields'. To get to Westminster you could go along the Strand from London, but the Exchequer and Privy Seal clerks, who worked at Westminster and usually lodged in London, often preferred, like many others, to go by water, especially in winter when the roads were so muddy. The River Thames was a fine highway, though the famous bridge, with houses on it, like the Ponte Vecchio still to be seen in Florence, was a dangerous hazard with its great supports which caused a six-foot drop in the water level when the tide was running strong. It also usually bore grim reminders of the rough punishments of the times, with its rotting heads of offenders stuck upon spikes. Within the city many houses had their gardens, often with vegetable plots and fruit-trees. The houses being mostly of no more than two storeys it must have been easy to see the blossoms in spring, and church towers every-where, with over all the gothic spire of Old St Paul's, destroyed in the seventeenth-century Great Fire of London. There were big mar-kets, and masses of shops, all governed by complex laws. There was a primitive sewage-system, arrangements for street-cleaning, a number of public latrines, and also much filth in the streets, with pigs routing about in the rubbish, and streams that were open sewers. It must have smelt like a farmyard in summer. No doubt Swift's famous poem 'On a City Shower', with all its disgust at squalor, would have described a true aspect of fourteenth-century London, though it was probably not so bad as eighteenth-century London. We do wrong, however, to estimate the city by our own standards of comfort and cleanliness; the truer and more natural view of it is as a remarkable achievement, with all its faults, in the art of living, won against heavy odds of physical difficulty in an age without machines; of administrative difficulty in an age when communication was slow and limited; of disciplinary difficulty in an age when Englishmen were violent, unruly and unstable as children; and of sheer difficulty of survival in an age of primitive medical science, ignorant of microbes. The English have rarely achieved a truly great city—perhaps few races have—but medieval London seems to have come as near to it as at any time. So at least thought one poet, writing in the later fifteenth century, when the city was much as it was in the later fourteenth century. I quote a modernised form of part of his poem (which was once attributed to Dunbar).

London, thou art of townés A *per se*,
Sovereign of cities, seemliest in sight. . . .

Above all rivers thy river hath renown,
Whose boreal streamés, pleasant and preclare,   *crystal; illustrious*
Under thy lusty wallés runneth down,
Where many a swan doth swim with wingés fair,
Where many a barge doth row and sail with air,
Where many a ship doth rest with top royal.
O town! of towns patron and not compeer;   *equal*
London, thou art the flower of cities all.

Upon the lusty bridge of pillars white
Be merchantés full royal to behold;
Upon thy streets goth many a seemly knight
In velvet gown and chainés of fine gold.
By Julius Caesar thy Tower founded of old
May be the house of Mars victorial,

Whose artillery with tongue may not be told;
London, thou art the flower of cities all.

Strong be thy wallés that about thee stands;
Wise be the people that within thee dwells;
Fresh is thy river with his lusty strands;
Blithe be thy churches; well sounding be thy bells;
Rich be thy merchantés in substance that excels;
Fair be thy wives, right lovesome, white and small:
Clear be thy virgins, lusty under kells;   *caps*
London, thou art the flower of cities all.

Thy famous Mayor, by princely governance,
With sword of justice thee ruleth prudently.
No Lord of Paris, Venice, or Florence
In dignity or honour goeth to him nigh;
He is exemplar, loadé-star and guy,   *guide*
Principal patron and rose original,
Above all Mayors as master most worthy;
London, thou art the flower of cities all.

Certainly there is a note of vulgar flattery here (the poem is said to
have been delivered at a city banquet), and a smug complacency not
at all un-English, even if the author was a Scot; but, comparisons
apart, what the author describes seems to have been genuinely true
of London.

The people who inhabited London and England in the fourteenth
century were conscious of being English as they had not been since
the Conquest. They recognised class-groupings, of course; those
who suffered from them, the lowest classes, wished them removed.
One of the demands of the rebellious peasants in 1381 was the abolition of serfdom, for the misery and bitterness of serfdom were enormous. However, the number of priests and the scattering of gentry
who were associated with the rising, on the one hand, and the ease

with which it was put down, on the other, together with the absence of serfdom in a number of counties, suggest that there was no fundamental split here, utterly dividing English society. It was becoming more possible for peasants to enrich themselves and to rise in society, even apart from the Church which had for long offered the chance of escape from the ignorant, sweated poverty which was the lot of the mass of the peasantry. Even a knight might have a serf as ancestor, while at the end of the century John Greyndor, a yeoman from the Forest of Dean, rose by his capacity as a ruthless captain (he beheaded 300 captives after a battle with the Welsh in 1405) to become Member of Parliament, sheriff of Glamorgan and of Gloucester, and constable of four border castles. This is exceptional, but it indicates the fluidity of movement between the classes of society which has always existed in England. Greyndor himself in later life turned merchant of Bristol (and was in fact guilty of something like piracy), and this is yet another example of the way in which, among the upper classes in England, trade and the professions (including that of war), merchants and the nobility, found it easy to mix. When Gaunt, the greatest noble in England (and about this time the most hated), was pursued by the mob in 1381, he was having dinner with a great merchant, Sir John Ypres. Sir John Montague, later Earl of Salisbury, was the third husband of a rich mercer's daughter. Nicholas Brembre, the grocer, was rich enough to make loans to Richard II and John of Gaunt. He was knighted for his bold behaviour during the Revolt, and was closely associated with the ruling court faction which was displaced by the barons in 1388. He paid for his social mobility and his financial and political power with death.

The upper classes, naturally, often resisted the movement from class to class, and Parliament in 1363 passed a 'sumptuary' law, regulating the food and clothing that each class should have. Naturally, it was not obeyed. A chronicler says that yeomen dress like squires, squires like knights, knights like dukes, and dukes like kings. Chaucer, in his description of those social climbers *par excellence*, the city merchants, or gildsmen, describes them, no doubt deliberately, as wearing clothing above their station.

All this shows that along with much unease (there were often riots in London), and much oppression, English society by the second half of the century was reasonably well united, if not harmonious. The old division between Norman-French and English had long been swept away. The legal distinction between a crime committed by an Englishman, and one committed by a Norman, introduced by William the Conqueror for holding down a defeated English nation with a small Norman-French force, had long been out of date when it was abolished by Parliament in 1340.

The clearest and most interesting example of the unification of the people lies in the common language, for a common language is the very lifeblood of community. After the Conquest the language of the King's court became French, and the language of administration was Latin or English. In the thirteenth century, after the loss of Normandy in 1204, French influence greatly increased, not least because the French language and French literature were the richest and most interesting in Europe. The real period of French domination in language was the second half of the thirteenth century and the first half of the fourteenth century. Yet there is good evidence that very soon after the Conquest English was the first language of all classes and the language that came naturally to them in extremity, for they learnt it from their mothers and their nurses. Norman knights married Englishwomen, often from the families whose estates they usurped. Ordericus Vitalis was the son of one of William's knights but born in England of an English mother. He was placed in a French monastery when a little boy and tells us of his sadness among strangers whose language he did not know. Ailred, the great English churchman of the twelfth century in the North, in youth a courtier at the Scottish King's court and therefore speaking French, author of many works in Latin, when he was on his deathbed prayed in English, like Bede four centuries before. When Edward I (1272-1307) was in danger of drowning he shouted mainly in English—'Oiyer nu (now)—I forga mi lyf'—and he was able to swear in English. When Henry, first Duke of Lancaster, wrote his devotional tract, *Le Livre de Seyntz Medicines*, in 1354, he used French, but says he is 'not much accustomed to French'. By the time of Richard II (1377-1400) the language of the court was English, as the whole of Chaucer's works and many other writings prove. At the end of the century some ambassadors sent to France knew no French at all and had to communicate in Latin.

The decisive change in education took place about the middle of the century. Higden, an historian writing about the time of Chaucer's birth, says that English children against the custom of all other nations are forced to leave their own language and construe their lessons (which were in Latin) into French. Gentlemen's children are taught French from their cradles, while rustic provincials try to learn French for its snob value. But when in 1385 Trevisa came to translate Higden's Latin (the translation itself showing the increasing power of English) he added the note that after the Black Death boys were taught in English instead of French, with the result that children of grammar school know no more French than 'their left heel', and even the children of gentlemen are not much taught it. Only a generally English education can account for the flowering of English literature in the rest of the century. The use of French in the law-courts was forbidden in 1362 because people could not understand it, though the records were still kept in French until the eighteenth century, and our law still keeps many French words. Parliament was opened in English for the first time in 1363, though French or Latin was more often used for the rest of the century.

English had yet to create a generally accepted standard, and there were many dialects in different parts of the country, but on the other hand there seems to have been no serious difficulty of understanding between one part and another. The first use of the idea of 'the King's English', though not the actual phrase, is by Chaucer himself, as we should expect, when he says, in the scientific work called *The Astrolabe*, written for his little son Lewis,

And pray God save the king, that is lord of this language.

Chaucer often refers to the English language, mentioning its changeableness, and the shortage of rhymes. French remained a powerful influence on English, and continued to give it new words for centuries. English did not achieve a complete triumph in all departments of life and thought (for instance, in science) until the eighteenth century. In Chaucer's time most courtiers, like Chaucer and Richard, must have known both French and English, and have been almost as much at home with French poetry as with English. English courtiers wrote poems in French. John Gower, who died in 1408, wrote one of his long poems in Latin, the next in French, and the third and last, the *Confessio Amantis*, in English. Richard's generation was certainly the last to be really familiar with French, and even for his generation English was established firmly as the national speech, at all levels, of a nationally self-conscious people.

A sense of national as well as personal identity depends on some feeling for and knowledge of the past. Even the poorer and uneducated people of England had a strong, if simple, historical sense, shown in the vigour with which they maintained ancient customs and status, often in the face of angry opposition from their masters. Memory of the Anglo-Saxon heritage seems never to have quite died out. The better educated had a more developed historical sense. Christianity being an 'historical' religion encourages some sense of the past. Monastic chroniclers were busy recording history from the Creation to the then present day. Within the general sense of history there seems to have been in the second part of the fourteenth century an upsurge of feeling about the specifically English past. It was a strong feeling of identity with the previous inhabitants of the land, even where there was little blood-relationship. Racialism hardly existed. The English interest in King Arthur is the most extreme example. In so far as Arthur was a real person he was a Romanised Celt who tried to resist the English invaders in the fifth century. Celtic mythology and pseudo-history, followed by French Romance, had made him, by the twelfth century, a model of chivalry who was the greatest king these islands had ever known. From the twelfth century onwards both English and the Norman-French conquerors in England took equal patriotic pride in Arthur. The Plantagenet kings down to Edward III and Richard II were felt to be his legitimate successors. It was believed that Arthur would return to help in time of national calamity, and a monk in Bodmin in the twelfth century who was rash enough to express his doubts of this was nearly lynched by the mob.

Arthur by no means displaced the memory of the English kings who were thought to have succeeded him before the Norman Conquest. The memory of Alfred's wisdom was sustained for centuries in the common speech by the proverbs that were attributed to him. But more particularly the upsurge of feeling about the English past is shown by the cult in Richard II's court of Edward the Confessor. With him should probably be associated Edmund the Martyr, for both these Anglo-Saxon royal saints are shown on the Wilton Diptych, together with John the Baptist, as sponsors of Richard II (see p. 190). Anglo-Saxon saints in general seem to have become popular about this time, and Chaucer mentions another Anglo-Saxon royal saint, the child Kenelm, in *The Nun's Priest's Tale*. In the North and West Midlands there was a renewed interest from the middle of the century onwards in poetry which descends directly from Anglo-Saxon poetry with its stern heroic temper and alliterative metre; and this is after three centuries of almost complete silence of such poetry. In general the resurgence of the English language which is so notable a characteristic of the later fourteenth century is one of the most important aspects of the new sense of national identity, of Englishness.

Not only did all classes feel that they were English; they were self-conscious about it, often rather pleased about it, though intellectuals were not. There was a new dislike of the foreigner. Higden, writing in the *Polychronicon* near the middle of the century, though also quoting older authorities, has this to say (I quote a modernised version of Trevisa's late fourteenth-century translation from Higden's Latin):

> The people of the south [of England] are easier and more mild; and men of the north are more unstable, more cruel, and more uneasy; the middle men are somewhat partners with both. Also they are accustomed to gluttony more than other men, and are more extravagant in food and drink and clothing. . . . These men are successful both on horse and on foot, able and ready to all manner of deeds of arms, and are accustomed to have the victory and the mastery in every fight, where no treason is walking. And they are curious and know well enough how to tell wonders and deeds that they have seen. Also they go in divers lands—hardly any people are richer in their own land or more gracious in far and in strange land. They can better win and get new than keep their own heritage; therefore it is that they are spread so wide and think that every other land is their own heritage. The men are able for all manner of cunning and intelligence [so says the translator, but Higden says 'able for all work'] but before the deed blundering and hasty, and more wise after the deed; and often they easily leave off what they have begun.[1]

Higden also talks of the discontentedness of the English. It is not very profound, but that it could be written at all indicates some-

---

[1] *Polychronicon*, Vol. II, pp. 167-9, edited by Churchill Babington, Rolls Series, 1869.

thing of the national character. Foreigners, then as now, naturally found that character irritating. The French despised the English belief in King Arthur and the prophet Merlin (though it is interesting to note that Chaucer shows himself a sceptic about Arthurian legend). To the French we were a byword for fickleness and treachery (as we were for Malory, writing in the middle of the fifteenth century). 'Perfidious Albion' has a long history. Froissart should have the last word, for he knew the country well, and liked and admired many Englishmen.

> I, the author of this history, was at Bordeaux when the Prince of Wales [i.e. the Black Prince] marched to Spain, and witnessed the great haughtiness of the English, who are affable to no other nation than their own; nor could any of the gentlemen of Gascony or Spain, though they had ruined themselves by their wars, obtain office or appointment in their own country; for the English said they were neither on a level with them, nor worthy of their society, which made the Gascons very indignant. . . .

It could almost be Mr E. M. Forster talking about the products of the English public schools.

Self-confidence, pride, even arrogance; the belief (as Froissart says) 'that they cannot lose', a certain readiness and energy, an openness to change and a quickness to practical experiment (as with the longbow that murdered the French chivalry), a high degree of efficiency when compared with other countries—these are obvious characteristics of Chaucer's countrymen. We might add some more. Cruel and violent as were the times, Englishmen even of the upper classes were less cruel and violent than men on the Continent; there was, for example, greater reluctance to use torture. On one occasion Froissart says the French nobles were worse than the English to the peasantry of France. For all their absurdities the English peasants when driven to revolt had a constructive plan of society, and for all their violence showed a sense of direction and a degree of responsibility that compares favourably with the much worse uprisings of the worse oppressed peasants in France. Life itself in England had plenty of recreation and beauty, and for all the horrors of plague, and for all the bad government of Richard's reign, finishing with his dethronement and murder, there is no sense of tired pessimism among all the satire and complaint. Whether this adds up to a truly 'merry England' it is perhaps impossible to say, but into this society, mirroring much of it, and sustained by it, was born one of the greatest humorists and most tender-hearted poets of the European tradition, Geoffrey Chaucer.

CHAPTER TWO

The Pride of Life

THE story of England in the time of Chaucer must begin with the story of her kings. Under a good king things went fairly well; under a bad one they went badly. Edward III came to the throne in 1327 at the age of fourteen, when his father, Edward II, was foully murdered at the instance of Mortimer, who then ruled with Edward's mother Isabella. At fifteen Edward was married to Philippa of Hainault. At seventeen he displaced Mortimer, and in spite of Isabella's pleading, had him hanged. Almost immediately he was engaged in an ill-advised war with the Scots, as he was to be frequently throughout his reign. While he was engaged in winning fruitless victories in Scotland, the French king, Scotland's ally, was stirring up trouble in Aquitaine and Gascony, the great area in France of which Bordeaux was the chief town, and which at that time owed obedience to the English king. There were also conflicts of trading interests between France and England in the Low Countries, and English and French traders were killing each other on the seas. But with all the other reasons for English enmity to France, no doubt Froissart has much of the truth of it when he says,

> The English will never love or honour their king, unless he be victorious and a lover of arms and war against their neighbours and especially such as are greater and richer than themselves. Their land is more fulfilled of riches and all manner of goods when they are at war than in times of peace. They take delight and solace in battles and slaughter: covetous and envious are they above measure of other men's wealth. . . . The King of England must needs obey his people and do their will.

Bodiam Castle, Sussex, 1386. Compare the walls with plate
Copyright Country Life

In the fourteenth and fifteenth centuries the general level of prosperity on the whole declined, and plunder was more than ordinarily attractive. And the English, though morally no worse than their neighbours for making war, were much better placed. Edward III was the ideal medieval king, and in 1337, with the advice of his Council, he declared war on France, a war which lasted on and off for about a hundred years. It is impossible to give any detailed account of it. Froissart fills hundreds of pages with the details of colourful arrays, bold adventures and fantastic bravery, burnings, slaughterings, desolation. It is painful to read how countrysides, at

Effigy of Edward III in Westminster Abbey

first rich, peaceful, and prosperous, were again and again ravaged; how unsuspecting communities were fallen upon, plundered and slaughtered. Froissart's description written after the Black Prince's expedition which included the battle of Poitiers is an example for all:

> The people were good and simple, who did not know what war was; indeed no war had been waged against them until the Prince came. The English and Gascons found the country full and gay, the rooms adorned with carpets and draperies, the caskets and chests full of fair jewels. But nothing was safe from these robbers. They, and especially the Gascons, who are very greedy, carried off everything.

When the Prince's men returned to Bordeaux their horses were so laden with booty they could scarcely move.

It was not quite all one-sided. As soon as war was declared, some French knights landed at Southampton one Sunday morning, whilst the inhabitants were at church; Normans, Picards, and Spaniards entered the town, pillaged it, killed or ill-treated the inhabitants, and having loaded their vessels with booty made sail for the coast of Normandy.

The war started slowly, with personal challenges delivered be-

Soldiers looting

tween outstanding knights, and with various individual raids by French and English, of the kind just described, which were such as that exquisite young man, Chaucer's Squire, had been engaged in:

And he hadde been somtyme in chyvachie,
In Flaundres, in Artoys, and Pycardie,
And born hym weel, as of so litel space,
In hope to stonden in his lady grace.

General Prologue, C.T. I, ll. 85-8

Such expeditions were regarded as worthy, gallant and glamorous. Froissart says, of two armies drawn up for battle, 'It was a fine sight to see the banners and pennons flying in the plain, the barbed horses, the knights and esquires richly armed.' In the earlier days of the war many ladies travelled to see the fighting and the tournaments and to take part in the feasting and the dancing. Among the English there was always an enthusiasm for the fighting in France. Soldiers were paid in wages (an innovation which suggests the non-feudal, national and efficient character of Edward's armies) and in loot, which added to their enthusiasm.

The first battle was the naval victory at Sluys, where the French

The English longbow

fleet was destroyed, largely by the English archers. The big success was the battle of Crécy in 1346, in which one of the leading formations was commanded by the Black Prince, aged sixteen. The victory was due to the brilliant tactical judgement of Edward, especially in his use of archers, and to the incompetence of the French. It was a period in warfare when attack was much inferior to defence, but in which the ideal of brave conduct was to hurl yourself on the foe. Edward chose his position well, protected by hedges, and on a low rise in the ground. The horsemen with their long lances were dismounted and set between the archers, to defend them against the shock of assault. The French were tired by a long approach march, but it was impossible to hold the knights back, each of them anxious to have the glory of the first assault. The vast numbers of the French cavalry became a disorganised horde. The French King ordered his 15,000 Genoese crossbowmen, despised mercenaries, to attack. The crossbow was weaker, though easier to handle, than the English longbow, and moreover the Genoese had got their bow-strings wet, while the English had kept their bowstrings dry in cases. The Genoese met a withering hail of English arrows, comparable for its effect with the small-arms fire of the English riflemen of the first year of the First World War. The wretched Genoese, out-ranged, were driven back in confusion, and the French King shouted, 'Kill me those scoundrels.' The French knights, pushed on by their comrades pressing from the rear, and enraged by the Genoese failure, rode in to the slaughter of their allies, while the arrows hailed down on them all. When the French men-at-arms eventually struggled up to the English lines they were attacked by the large numbers of Welsh and Cornish footmen whom Edward had with him. These brave Celtic footmen were armed with large knives, with which they hamstrung the horses. They also knifed unhorsed knights lying on the ground unable to move because of their heavy armour, 'at which', says Froissart, 'the King of England was after much exasper-ated', for apart from the fellow-feeling among European chivalry, a captured knight was worth a large sum for ransom. The con-fusion and slaughter among the French army are indescribable. There are many stories of individual gallantry, including that of the blind King of Bohemia on the French side. He asked his companions, as he was blind, to lead him into the battle that he might strike one stroke with his sword. His gentlemen fastened all the reins of their horses together, with their king at the head. They were all found dead together the next day, with their horses still tied together. The Prince of Wales was himself hard pressed at one time, and one of his knights rode off to Edward, who was commanding the tactical reserve, to ask for help. The King asked if his son were dead, unhorsed, or so badly wounded that he could not support himself. 'No, thank God,' said the knight. Froissart, who tells the story, continues,

The King answered, 'Now, Sir Thomas, return back to those that sent you, and tell them from me, not to send again for me this day, or expect that I shall come, let what will happen, as long as my son has life; and say, that I command them to let the boy win his spurs; for I am determined, if it please God, that all the glory and honour of this day shall be given to him, and to those into whose care I have entrusted him.' The knight returned to his lords, and related the King's answer, which mightily encouraged them, and made them repent they had ever sent such a message.

His Lady hands the Knight his war-helm

It is such stories as this, combined with his successes, that show how Edward held the hearts of his subjects, and which account for the national self-confidence that he created during his reign. And surely, the reliance on the king, the capacity for organisation, the responsibility and bravery of the men in the Peasants' Revolt, was something learnt on the battlefields of Europe by the archers on whose skill, discipline and steadfastness the victories were founded. The peasants' violence, too, was encouraged by their experience in war, for in the next couple of days the English put to the sword all whom they met.

In the next year Calais was starved into surrender, and there are two more stories, again from Froissart, which well illustrate the temper of the king and the times. When the governor of Calais

An assault on a castle

saw the preparations for the siege, he collected together all the poorer inhabitants, who had not been able to lay in any food, and one Wednesday morning sent more than seventeen hundred men, women, and children, out of the town.

> As they were passing through the English Army, they asked them, why they had left the town? They replied, because they had nothing to eat. The King, upon this, allowed them to pass through in safety, ordered them a hearty dinner, and gave to each two sterlings, as charity and alms, for which many of them prayed earnestly for the King.

Such incidental softenings of the multiple horrors of war are almost always due to the Christian teachings of the age, and one can only wish, as in all ages, that they had been more frequent and more radical. The other more famous story again illustrates the mercy, and also the temperamental behaviour of such people as Edward; it is the famous story of the burghers of Calais. The king offered not to put the whole town to the sword if six of the chief men would give themselves up unconditionally. With great gallantry six of the leading *bourgeois* offered themselves to Edward, and asked for mercy. All the knights and barons around Edward wept for pity, but he was furious because of the losses suffered at sea from the people of Calais, and, disregarding all the pleas of his own knights, he ordered the hostages to be executed. Queen Philippa was with him, big with child, and she fell on her knees with tears to plead for them, 'for the sake of the Son of the Blessed Mary, and for your love to me'. Edward gave way, but his mercy was reluctant, and his terms harsh. He evacuated all the French, and repeopled Calais with English.

There was a truce, and not much fighting in the north of France until the big expedition of 1359-60, when Chaucer took part and was captured, and this was concluded by the treaty of Bretigny. In the centre of France the Black Prince conducted the cruel and profitable raids which included the battle of Poitiers (1356) where a much outnumbered English force, which, laden with loot, would have preferred not to fight, repeated the tactics and victory of Crécy, and captured the French King himself. The Black Prince, who when he later took Limoges massacred the whole population, turning his face from pleading women and children, waited humbly on the captured King, standing behind his chair at supper, and praising his chivalry. King John was taken with high honour back to England, and a huge ransom demanded for him.

To celebrate the victory of Crécy and the fall of Calais Edward elaborated an idea that had been growing for some time, and which was typical of the age. He instituted an order of chivalry, based on the idea of King Arthur and the knights of the Round Table. By all Englishmen of the fourteenth century (except, it would seem, the cynical Chaucer) it was believed that Arthur had truly existed and was the greatest of English kings. Most of the courtly and chivalrous literature of the French language was based on the Arthurian legends, which indeed the French had done most to elaborate. Edward's Order was that of the Garter, and it now seems possible that the old story of how the young Countess of Salisbury, with whom the King was then in love, dropped her garter at a ball in Calais, and how the king picked it up, binding the blue ribbon round his knee, is indeed true. As he did so he spoke the words which with sublime inconsequence became the Garter motto: 'Honi soit qui mal y pense'—Evil be [to him] who thinks evil of this.

It seems possible that the Countess of Salisbury was a lady with a rather curious history. She may have been Joan Plantagenet, the younger daughter of Edmund of Woodstock, Earl of Kent, sixth son of Edward I. Joan, later known as Joan of Kent, who was born in 1328, was first cousin to Edward III, though fifteen years younger. When she was two Mortimer had her father executed, and according to Froissart the young Queen Philippa took charge of her. She grew up to be, according again to Froissart, 'the most beautiful woman in England, and the most loving, famous for her beauty and the

extravagance of her dress'. William Montague, second Earl of Salisbury, and his steward, Sir Thomas Holland, each of them so distinguished as to be among the founder members of the Order of
the Garter, both fell in love with her. Holland brought about a
marriage-contract, and she became his wife in or about 1340, when
she was twelve. Then he went away to the French wars, and in his
absence Salisbury went through a form of marriage with her about
a year or two later. It is unfortunate that of this and other changes
of fortune the lady's opinion is not recorded, but it is evident that
all her life she was of a peace-loving disposition. Holland, who
made a fortune in the war from the capture of an important prisoner,
eventually had enough money to petition the Pope to have his wife
restored. Salisbury imprisoned Joan to hinder the suit, but eventually the Pope decided against him and in favour of Holland in 1349.
After the early death of her two brothers Joan became Countess of
Kent in her own right. By Holland she had three sons and two
daughters, but he died in 1360, when she was thirty-two. Within
nine months the Prince of Wales had fallen in love with her and
married her, thereby spoiling several of Edward's schemes for a possible diplomatic marriage of the Prince with a foreign princess. There
was nothing surprising in the speed with which she remarried. In
times of roughness, especially for a rich widow, unprotected from
male aggressiveness, it was entirely usual. She had two sons by the
Black Prince; Edward, who died at the age of five, much to his
father's grief, and Richard, who later became King. She looked
after Richard until Edward died in 1377, and she was notable as a
peacemaker between Gaunt and the angry Londoners. She was
very much at the centre of affairs. Several of her knights were important in Richard's court, and several of them were among the
famous 'Lollard knights', of whom more later. She must have
known Chaucer, and it has been suggested that it is she who is
figured as Alcestis in the *Prologue* to *The Legend of Good Women*,

though there is no certain evidence. There is a story that she was met by a band of peasants on the road during the Revolt in 1381, and that they forced her to kiss them. In those later years she became fat, but when trouble broke out between Richard and one of his half-brothers, the extremely violent and unpleasant Sir John Holland, and Richard threatened to have him executed, she travelled frequently and painfully to bring about a reconciliation between them. Her apparent failure to do so was thought to have brought on her death, in 1385. Her former husband, Salisbury, remained about the court for the rest of a long life, without embarrassment or resentment. He had a career of distinguished military service, and soon after losing Joan married the daughter of one of the other founder-members of the Garter, by whom he had one son, William. William married a daughter of the Earl of Arundel (there was a network of interrelationships and marriages among the great families) but was accidentally killed in a tournament by his own father in 1382.

To return to the Order of the Garter in 1348. Apart from King Edward and the Black Prince some of the other members were men whose names occur like continuous threads throughout any account of the time. First among the founder-members after the King and the Prince is Henry Plantagenet, Earl of Derby, Duke of Lancaster, whom I shall call for convenience Henry of Lancaster, by the title he eventually received in 1352. He was a cousin of King Edward, and was born early in the fourteenth century. He was early one of the most prominent courtiers, and distinguished himself in the Scottish and the French wars for his generalship, for being always in the forefront of the actual fighting, and also for his powers of negotiation. In 1352 he arranged to go on one of the crusades against the Lithuanian pagans, and the King of France arranged for Otto, Duke of Brunswick, to arrest him on the way. Henry continued nevertheless, but found that a truce had been arranged and there was no fighting to be done. On his return he complained of the Duke of

Brunswick and a duel was arranged. Having obtained permission from Edward he left England with one earl and sixty knights in his train, with their esquires and horses and equipment. When he met the Duke of Brunswick in the lists the duke was overcome with terror and abjectly apologised. The King of France, John the Good, entertained Henry most courteously, and would have given him many rich gifts, but he would only accept a thorn out of the Saviour's crown, which he deposited in the collegiate church of Our Lady in Leicester. This was only the high peak of his career in the tournament, for he was exceedingly fond of jousting. Froissart and other chroniclers tell a number of stories of his bravery, courtesy, generosity, kindness, and rather sardonic humour. On one occasion, the King of France, then Philippe of Valois, beheaded the Lord of Clisson, because he thought him favoured by the English. Edward in a rage wished to behead another Frenchman, his prisoner, in revenge, but Henry of Lancaster dissuaded Edward from so dishonourable an act, and moreover took into his own guardianship the two children of the Lord of Clisson. Henry was no war-monger. When the Treaty of Bretigny was drawn up in 1360, and Edward was very reluctant to accept the terms offered by the French, it was Henry who persuaded him. He died of the pestilence in 1361. His second daughter and his heir was Blanche, who married Edward's son John of Gaunt, and who herself died in the next great pestilence of 1367. It was through her that John of Gaunt became Duke of Lancaster, 'time-honoured Lancaster', and it was their son, another Henry, who after becoming Earl of Derby and Earl of Lancaster, finally became Henry IV of England. Chaucer must have known Henry of Lancaster, at least remotely, and it was the death of his daughter Blanche which was the occasion of Chaucer's *Book of the Duchess*.

Henry of Lancaster was the richest man in the kingdom; his daily expenditure was the fantastic sum of £100; with all his other virtues of birth, person, mind and character it is not surprising that praise of him was unanimous and high. Like Chaucer's knight he was both worthy and wise, loving truth, honour and courtesy, and no one in the whole century comes nearer to the chivalric ideal.

This paragon has yet another claim to our interest. He wrote a deeply sincere and often beautiful devotional tract called the Book of Holy Medicines, *Le Livre de Seyntz Medicines*, only recently discovered by Dr Arnould,[1] which shows the devoutness, humility and self-reproach which inspired this great gentleman. It is one of the earliest signs of the new spirituality among lay Englishmen that became more and more evident as the century progressed, and of which Chaucer and several of his friends are good examples. Henry's chief difference is that being of a slightly earlier generation he wrote in French not English. The tract shows a fine religious sensibility, self-reproachful and idealistic but not in the least neurotic or morbid. It is also unusually vivid, with many fresh realistic illustrations from ordinary life. Although the circumstances are so different the tone reminds one of the devotional writings of that later member of a noble family, George Herbert, and both might be quoted as examples of a high aristocratic religious sensibility that seems peculiarly English, and indeed—theology apart—Anglican.

Another founder-member of the Order of the Garter was Sir John Chandos, the son of landed gentry of Norman blood, whose estate was on the Welsh border. He was perhaps the most famous of all English knights, with gallant achievements in almost every military expedition in thirty years, the inseparable companion of the Black Prince and always his faithful servant and adviser. He too, though so brave a fighting-man, was renowned for his generalship, and has to his name a number of acts of mercy. Had the Black Prince followed his advice and refrained from taxing the inhabitants of Aquitaine so cruelly the course of history might have been dif-

[1] Henry of Lancaster, *Le Livre de Seyntz Medicines*, ed. by E. J. Arnould, The Anglo-Norman Text Society, 1940.

ferent. Like Henry of Lancaster and other nobles he was a founder of religious institutions, but he is not known to have written anything.

Another Garter knight, though not quite a founder-member, was Sir Walter Manny, friend of Chandos and Henry of Lancaster, and one whose life was full of chivalric adventures. His family was from Hainault, part of modern Belgium, and he was one of Queen Philippa's esquire-carvers. In 1337 he rescued Henry of Lancaster who had been struck down in battle, and he is said to have excelled everyone in the sea-battle of Sluys. On one occasion the King and the Black Prince fought, disguised as plain knights, under his banner. He was high in the councils of the King. When he died he was buried in the London Charterhouse of which, with the Bishop of London, he was co-founder. He also had two illegitimate daughters, unkindly named Mailosel (perhaps meaning May-wanton) and Malplesant (ill-pleasing), who both became nuns.

Other knights of the Garter who are of interest here for their parts in war and politics and associations with Chaucer were of a later generation than the founder-members. They were such men as Sir Lewis Clifford, who carried a complimentary poem from the French poet Deschamps to Chaucer, and who was one of those knights associated with Lollardy; Sir Simon Burley, one of the tutors of Richard II and a leader of the court faction with which Chaucer had some associations; Sir William Beauchamp, associated with another faction, but with whom also Chaucer had some relationship; Sir John Montagu, third Earl of Salisbury, and a Lollard; and Sir Philip de la Vache, son-in-law of Sir Lewis Clifford, to whom Chaucer wrote his short poem *Truth*.

In many respects the foundation of the Order of the Garter marks the high peak of Edward's successes. Nothing went quite so well, at home or abroad, after that. Yet the period of success consolidated the English nation and gave it the force and self-confidence that helped to carry it through all the difficulties, miseries, and follies of the rest of the century. The beginnings of an effective administration, the foundation of a brilliant court, were also among the achievements of Edward, and in these the Order of the Garter surely played a great part. It bound to the sovereign by the closest ties of honour, friendship and interest a good selection of the most powerful and able men of the kingdom, each of them by turn soldier, courtier, diplomat and administrator. The gaiety of the annual feasts on St George's day, the issue of splendid robes, the feasting, dancing, tournaments, was an outward expression of the inner unity of the Order, maintained even when a few of its members were condemned for rebellion at the end of the century. Both in ceremony and political usefulness it was typical of Edward's genius as a medieval king for sharing and joining to himself the enthusiasms of his subjects. His grandson Richard II, with his disregard for other people, his egotism and wilful favouritism, could never have created such an institution, and it speaks well for Edward's sureness of touch, as well as for the continuity of English culture, that of all the orders of knighthood created in Europe at about that time the Garter alone survives till the present day.

There is a scrap of contemporary description of Edward, and his son, the Black Prince, and of the garter-decoration, which brings in a touch of colour. It comes in the western alliterative political poem *Winner and Waster*, written about 1350. The poet in a dream sees a pavilion on the crest of a hill, all adorned in red, both roof and sides, and bright with English gold coins, each one gaily circled with garters of Indian blue plentifully embroidered with gold. Each garter has worked above it the motto in English 'Scorn have the man who thinks any harm' (a version of *Honi soit qui mal y pense*). A man (the Black Prince) stands by the pavilion, made like a satyr, with curly hair, with a helmet, and on the helmet a covering, and on the covering a vigorous leopard—the leopard of the arms of England. It looks very bravely, made of yellow and gold in a lively way. The covering has the leopards of England and the lilies of France on it, and is adorned with pearl in each corner. Then the poet sees a comely king, crowned with gold, sitting on a bench covered with silk, a sceptre in his hand. He is one of the loveliest men you could ever see. He wears a kirtle and mantle as berry-brown as his beard and embroidered with birds, fine gold falcons flapping their wings, each one bearing a great garter of Indian blue. He also wears a bright belt embroidered with birds, drakes and ducks that seem to be trembling for fear of the falcons.

These descriptions may well symbolise the pride—and the danger —of life. It is also to the point that the rest of the poem is engaged in showing, under heraldic imagery, some of the political and economic problems of the age.

Effigy of the Black Prince in Canterbury Cathedral

CHAPTER THREE

Times of Stress

THOUGH it may have been thought of earlier, the Garter was probably regularly founded in 1348. In the same year, with the contrast the period is rich in, began the Great Pestilence, or, as it has since come to be called, the Black Death. An anonymous English chronicler writes:

> And in this same year, and in the year before, and also in the year after, was so great a pestilence of men [come] from the East into the West, and specially through ulcers, that he that sickened on this day, died on the third day after. To the which men that so died in this pestilence, that had but little respite of lying ill, the Pope Clement, of his goodness and grace, gave them full remission and forgiving of all their sins that they were shriven of. And this pestilence lasted in London from Michaelmas [i.e. 29th September] into August next following, almost a whole year. And in these days was death without sorrow, wedding without friendship, wilful penance, and dearth without scarcity, and fleeing without refuge or succour, for many fled from place to place because of the pestilence; but they were infected, and might not escape the death.

There is still much mystery surrounding the progress and effects of this dreadful disease, which was very painful and accompanied by delirium. One chronicler says that hardly a tenth part of the people was left alive; another says that almost the whole population of Bristol died, and gives other examples of the terrible mortality. These are exaggerations, but even the latest conservative estimate gives an average loss over the whole country of one fifth of the population, while the clergy lost about a half of their numbers. By the end of the century it is thought that the population, from this and later visitations of the Plague, may have been half of what it was at the beginning of the century.

The immediate result was a shortage of goods and labour which (after a catastrophic fall of prices during the plague itself) led to much increased prices, and the attempt by landlords to enforce again the labour services from serfs which had begun to be given up for money payments. Parliament passed laws, the Statutes of Labourers, insisting that wages should be kept down to what they were before the Plague. The result was labour unrest which, with other causes, came to a climax in the Peasants' Revolt.

In 1359-60 Edward III made his last invasion of France. France was prostrate, but militarily speaking Edward was unlucky and did well to conclude, by Henry of Lancaster's advice, the Treaty of Bretigny, by which Edward retained lordship over Aquitaine and Gascony, with other lands, the town of Calais and its environs, and received the first vast instalment of the ransom of the French King John, who was set free.

The Prince of Wales was then sent to govern Aquitaine. There he became involved with the struggle of the ruling family of Castile, and he supported with excessive generosity the exiled monarch who is now known, with excellent reason, as Pedro the Cruel. Pedro had been excommunicated, and his illegitimate brother Henry the Bastard had seized the throne. When Pedro appealed to the Black Prince for aid, even the Gascons wished to refuse it, but, said the Black Prince of Pedro's dethronement, 'All kings and sons of kings should never agree to it, for it is a great blow at the royal state.' Although Pedro was dishonest as well as cruel, and went back on his promise to pay for the military help the Black Prince provided, this was perhaps the sort of behaviour not unexpected in a king; certainly Edward III was not guiltless, and ruined his bankers. At all events, in 1371, the Black Prince's brother, John of Gaunt, married

Pedro's daughter and assumed in her right the title of King of Castile
—castles in Spain! Chaucer gives the official English view of Pedro
(the more naturally as his wife was for a time lady-in-waiting to
Pedro's daughter in England) when, in commenting on his death he
calls him 'O noble, O worthy Petro, glorie of Spain'. Chaucer is
so extraordinary a mixture of the conservative and the careless, the
orthodox and the free-thinking, that one would dearly like to know
his true private opinion. But the idea of true private opinion hardly
existed, and personal expression was rare. Yet even Chandos Herald,
in the poem I shall now quote, says that Pedro was not as loyal as
the Prince thought.

On behalf of Pedro the Black Prince invaded Spain in 1367 and
won for him the great victory of Nájera. It was a very typical
battle, and though militarily and politically a waste of time, it has
much interest for us in that it was well described about 1385 for the
English court in French verse by an eye-witness, the herald of the
famous knight, Sir John Chandos. Many of Chaucer's friends and
acquaintances took part; Gaunt himself, Sir Guichard d'Angle, Sir
William Beauchamp, and others. They prayed devoutly at the beginning of the battle.

On the field the Duke of Lancaster said to William Beauchamp,
'See, there are our enemies. But so help me Jesus Christ, today you
shall see me a good knight if death does not hinder me.' Then he said,
'Forward, forward banner! Let us take the Lord God for our Pro-
tector, and let each one aquit himself honourably.' The noble and
valiant duke placed himself before all his men; more than a hundred he
made bolder-hearted than they were before. . . . There might one see
the companions coming, all close together, banners and pennons. Each
one held lance in hand, and they made fierce onslaught to attack their
enemies. The archers kept on shooting. . . . Great were the din and
reek. There was neither banner nor pennon that was not cast down.
At one time that day Chandos was thrown to the ground; and upon
him fell a Castilian, a large man named Martin Fernandez, who strove

desperately to slay him, and wounded him through the vizor. Chandos boldly took a dagger from his side and thrust his sharp blade into the Castilian's body. The Castilian stretched himself out dead, and Chandos leapt to his feet. He grasped his sword with both hands and plunged into the fray, which was fierce and terrible and marvellous to behold. . . . Elsewhere the noble Duke of Lancaster, filled with valour, fought so nobly that everyone marvelled . . . neither did the Prince falter, but hastened to the battle. The battlefield was on a fair and beautiful plain, whereon was neither bush nor tree for a full league around, along a fine river, very rapid and fierce, which caused the Castilians much damage that day. . . . More than two thousand were drowned there. . . . My lords, the time I am telling you of was on a Saturday, the third day of April, when sweet and gentle birds begin to renew their songs in meadows, woods, and fields. It was at that time that the great battle of Nájera occurred, just as you have heard.

That night the Prince occupied the very lodging in which King Henry himself [his enemy] had been the night before. There they held high revel and thanked God the Father, the Son, and his blessed Mother for the grace he had done them, for you must know that they found there at once wine and bread—all the camp was well furnished therewith—coffers, vessels, gold and silver, whereat many people were pleased.[1]

This is the court poetry which Chaucer's must be compared with. Chaucer is much the better poet, but both he and his poetry must have lacked the special prestige of narratives like this. He may himself have heard the poem, surrounded by the very heroes whose names are mentioned in it. Here is seen that bravery in battle which is not described by Chaucer but is attributed by him to his hero Troilus, whom sometimes modern readers are inclined to think is childishly miserable and feeble. And there seems little reason to doubt that these bold warriors may well have behaved like Troilus or indeed like Edward himself, when they were stricken with love.

[1] Chandos Herald, *Life of the Black Prince*, ed. and transl. by M. K. Pope and E. C. Lodge, The Clarendon Press, Oxford, 1910, pp. 161 ff.

(At the same time, of course, we must make some allowance for literary exaggeration and court flattery in the account of the battle.)

The Spanish campaign was ultimately disastrous. The Black Prince there picked up the wasting disease that killed him nearly ten years later, and he was always a sick and irritable man afterwards. Pedro's default, and the Prince's own extravagance left him short of money to pay his troops. The taxes that he imposed in Aquitaine led to great unrest, war with France broke out again, and when another truce was finally made in 1375 only Calais, Bordeaux, and a few other towns remained in English hands of all the wide lands they had won.

While in the seventies things went badly in the war abroad, they also went very badly at home. The King became lazy and senile, and completely under the dominance of his mistress, Alice Perrers. Queen Philippa had died in 1369, one of the most gracious of English queens, a devoted wife and mother, patron of learning, an influence for good and mercy. Alice Perrers had become one of her ladies-in-waiting some time before 1366. In 1373 Edward gave Alice most of his late wife's jewels, besides many other grants of land and money before and after that date. Although she was not beautiful she is said to have had a blandishing tongue, and a feminine taste in lapdogs and embroidered gloves. She must also have had a brilliant and forceful personality. In 1375 she rode through the city from the Tower dressed as the Lady of the Sun on her way to attend the great jousts held in the wide space provided by Smithfield Market. She was accused of having forced herself on to the bench of judges at Westminster in order to influence cases in her favour. It has been suggested that Langland's portrait of Lady Meed [Bribery] is a hit at Alice:

[I] was aware of a woman, worthily clothed
Purfiled with pelure, the finest upon earth,   *trimmed with fur*
Crowned with a crown, the king hath none better.

43

Fetisly her fingers were fretted with gold wire,   *neatly; adorned*
And there-on red rubies, as red as any gleed,   *red-hot coal*
And diamonds of dearest price, and double manner of sapphires,
Orientals and ewages, envenoms to destroy.   *oriental sapphires; beryls*
Her robe was full rich, of red scarlet ingrained,
With ribbons of red gold, and of rich stones;
Her array me ravished, such richness saw I never;
I had wonder what she was, and whose wife she were.

Piers Plowman, B II, ll. 8-18

So may the Lady of the Sun indeed have looked. There is also some doubt about 'whose wife she were', but it seems that by 1376 she was married or at least contracted to a certain William de Windsor. She was attacked by the Good Parliament in 1376, and Edward is represented as saying that he did not know she was married, and asking his faithful commons to deal gently with her. In the next year she regained her influence, and was associated with Sir Richard Stury and Lord Latimer, both knights of Joan of Kent and Lollards, in attacks on Sir Peter de la Mare, the Speaker of the Good Parliament (and the first speaker recorded of any Parliament), who ended up in prison for his boldness. Alice was a powerful patron. Even Gaunt did not despise her services, nor did the bishop Wykeham when he wished to reinstate himself after a political setback. She also protected Richard Lyons, the monopolist, who at the time of the Good Parliament is said to have sent the Black Prince (who returned it) a bribe of a thousand pounds in a barrel for protection from Parliament's attacks. When Edward lay mortally ill in 1377 she cheered up the terrified old man by telling him he was not dying. The monk-chronicler Walsingham (whose abbey was disputing the ownership of property with her) tells us she kept Edward's confessor away till the last hours, then stole Edward's rings and deserted him before he died, speechless, but kissing the crucifix. Edward died of a stroke, and his funeral image in wax, still preserved in Westminster

Abbey, shows him as he lay on his last day, with one side of his face twisted. Richard's first Parliament again attacked Alice and extracted some of her riches, and again she fought back with some success. Her later years were full of litigation, including an outrageous lawsuit against Wykeham, which failed. She had lost her influence, and died in 1400.

In 1377, with a ten-year-old king, things looked black, though it may remind one of the enormous variety of life, and the complex tangle of many men's individual lives that make up the whole web, to reflect that the same period was for Chaucer himself a time of increasingly prosperous and busy occupation. Between 1370 and 1386 he produced a number of masterpieces which, if they have elements of tragedy, are also shot through with subtle humour. He was employed on important missions to Italy and France; he was appointed Comptroller of Customs, though this was no doubt something of a sinecure, and was appointed Knight of the Shire to represent Kent in the Parliament of 1386. In all this he was associated with some of the most important men of the age. His wife was lady-in-waiting to the Spanish wife of Gaunt, and his sister-in-law became Gaunt's mistress. Though never one of Gaunt's retainers himself, he received presents from Gaunt on occasions such as Christmas, and Gaunt was the greatest lord in the land under the King. At the Customs Chaucer acted as a check on the collectors, who no doubt did the actual work through their subordinates, and his collectors were those merchants, Walworth, Brembre, Philipot, whose power, through their wealth and influence in the city councils, was equal to, or more than, that of many a lord. In his missions his companions were such men as Sir Guichard d'Angle, one of the King's tutors, a gay, elderly and much-respected Gascon; Sir Richard Stury, one of the inner circle of government for very many years; Sir Thomas Percy, later the Earl of Worcester who helped Henry IV to power; Sir John Burley, another 'chamber knight', that is, one of the King's inner circle; Sir Lewis Clifford, friend of the famous French poet Deschamps, and the most trusted knight of Joan of Kent. Several of them were K.G.s. Not all can have been personal friends, and perhaps Chaucer was always in some sense in an inferior position, socially and politically, although he was the famous poet as well as the trusted courtier and diplomat. Most of these aquaintances, and others who might be mentioned, were in some way associated with the Lancastrian faction of Gaunt, or with what has been called 'the court party', but the political relationships of this small, competitive, sometimes savage society were so complex and so liable to shift, that it is not surprising that Chaucer in his published writings never ventures an opinion, save the most orthodox generality, on the needs and temper of the times. In the upheaval caused by the Merciless Parliament of 1388 the leader of the court party, Sir Simon Burley, and Brembre were both executed. Politics was a dangerous game, especially for those who, like Sir Simon Burley, Richard Stury, and other chamber knights, were making their fortune at it, and had not the protection of a great name and a large feudal retinue. Even for those who had such advantages there were risks, especially under Richard. Thomas of Woodstock was Earl of Gloucester and the King's own uncle, but that did not save him from being, as far as can be gathered, murdered in prison at his royal nephew's instigation.

In 1377, such events were only distant possibilities. There were larger black clouds looming nearer. The wars in France, Spain, and Scotland, though intermittent, were going badly. People were discontented with failure, and even more with the taxes that were needed for what seemed to them an inefficiently conducted war. The higher clergy were suspicious of the government, and of its insistence on the need for money. The city of London, on whose goodwill depended much of the government's ability to raise money, was also in uneasy relations with the government. The Commons in Parliament distrusted the government when it was run by bishops and when it was not; it saw the war going badly, and did not want to vote money. The whole state of the country was alarming, for labour troubles were increasing, and were made worse by the poll-taxes, often unjustly graded, which the Commons (who were mostly landed gentry) imposed on all. Underneath ran deeper cross-currents. There was a very general dislike of the Church, aroused by the spectacle of a rich institution whose high officers, the bishops, were often either government administrators or foreigners, and in either case absentees. Some of this anti-clericalism was mere greed for loot, some of it was political and patriotic, some of it was the result of taking the Bible's praise of poverty seriously. More laymen of all ranks could read, and that intense wish to feed on the biblical text which has had so profound an effect on English life, saw its birth in the latter part of the fourteenth century, in the Lollard movement.

It is not easy to say briefly exactly what Lollardy was, and more is said about it in the last chapter. Anti-clericalism inspired by read-ing the Bible was a part of it. It was never a simple movement, especially in the 1370's and 1380's, before it hardened into a perse-cuted movement with a programme. Nineteenth-century historians regarded it as the first stirring of the Reformation, and though this view has been disputed, it still seems to me to be the right one. In Chaucer's time people of all ranks were attracted to Lollardy, though in the fifteenth century, after the ill-conceived and unsuc-cessful Lollard revolt by Sir John Oldcastle in 1414, it lost almost all its upper-class adherents. Sharply persecuted, it became an under-ground movement mostly kept going by poor and simple and brave men. In this way it persisted till the sixteenth century, when it emerged, as scholars have recently shown, as part of the Reforma-tion. In its earliest stages Lollardy seems to have been a rationalistic questioning on the part of many lay people of the excessive ritual that overlay Christian worship; a questioning of the power of words

47

to turn the bread and wine of the Mass into the Real Presence of God; a denial of the magical virtues attributed to the statues or images of saints; a desire to approach God directly, without the interposition of priests; and consequently a desire that everyone should be able to read the Bible for himself in his own language. Not all these points were heretical, and many people inside the Church might be sympathetic to some or all of them. Wycliffe, whose life and teachings are discussed later, gave Lollardy an intellectual backbone, while at the same time powerful men like John of Gaunt thought they might make use of him for their own devious political purposes. When Wycliffe's teachings became extremely heretical, Gaunt dropped him. Lollardy was dangerous because it directly threatened the Church as an institution, and the Church was very much bound up with other social institutions, like the ownership of land and the right to labour-services, which were at the very heart of medieval society. When this became clear, it was natural that Lollardy should lose most of its upper-class members. It was not so clear in the 1370's and '80's, when it reflected a widespread religious stirring in the country, an important intellectual crisis which is still little understood, and a landmark in the development of the lay spirit.

Another disturbing movement, this time with its roots deep in the developing social structure of medieval England, was a general upsurge of 'smaller', less important men, against powerful ruling groups or persons. This can be seen in many walks of life, and was a result, perhaps, of the greater self-confidence and independence encouraged by the wars, as well as of such broader movements as the cumulative effects of education. The Commons exerted themselves against the Lords and the King's Council. In London the leaders of the smaller gilds rebelled against the monopoly of power among the leaders of the few large gilds. In the countryside the peasants rebelled against the lawyers and officials of repressive government, against the universally unpopular John of Gaunt, and against land-owning monasteries. Even Chaucer himself illustrates this compli-cated upsurge, for he was a literate, devout layman of a new kind, a court official of a new kind, not a fighter and not of gentle blood.

For a moment, for all the foreboding aroused by having a boy-king, the coronation and events surrounding it, superbly stage-managed by Gaunt, brought a peaceful lull. Gaunt brought about some dramatic reconciliations between himself and various enemies, with modest declarations and kneelings and kissings of each other and of the young King's hand. The coronation procession moved with customary splendour through the city to Westminster, and the people greeted it with enthusiasm. There must have been some-thing deeply touching in the sight of the fair-haired boy 'as fair as Absalom' moving among the great nobles of the realm. Walsing-ham no doubt spoke for all when he wrote, 'It was a day of joy and gladness . . . the long-awaited day of the renewal of peace and of the laws of the land, long exiled by the weakness of an aged king and the greed of his courtiers and servants.'

But the various strains of society were not to be so easily set at rest. Troubles came from within and without, and then in 1381 came the Peasants' Revolt. Even now it raises passions among his-torians; its causes are complex, the literature on it is large, and there can be no possibility of giving here anything like a full account. Since all those contemporaries who left any record were, by the very fact of being able to write, members of the threatened classes, they speak of it with horror and indignation. The poet Gower, Chaucer's friend, compares the peasants to enraged animals, while he compares terror-stricken fellow-landlords to wild beasts lurking in the woods, feeding on grass and acorns and wishing they could shrink into the bark of the trees. Though the rebels must have surged round the very gate, Aldgate, which Chaucer lived over, the only comment on this shattering event in his writings is a joking remark about Jack

Straw and his company chasing Flemings in *The Nun's Priest's Tale*.
But one of his moralising poems, *Lack of Steadfastness*, addressed to
Richard (giving advice to Richard being almost a national hobby
towards the end of the century) advises him to

Shew forth thy swerd of castigacioun   *punishment*

and Chaucer's personal views on the Revolt are unlikely to have
been other than orthodox.

Yet the peasants themselves were in some respects only putting
into practice the medieval Christian teaching of centuries. It is to
be noted that as well as a few gentry there were also a number of
parsons in their ranks. And for twenty years the hedge-priest John
Ball had been going about asking that famous question

When Adam delved and Eva span
Who was then the gentleman?

This was orthodox medieval Christian thought, though as always
there was often a deep gulf between thought and practice. It was
a commonplace repeated by Dante in Italy, Jean de Meun in France,
and Chaucer in England, that the only true nobility came from
virtue, not from descent, though one could hardly expect heralds to
apply such a test when a knight wished for a coat of arms. Tension
between virtue, class and inheritance is built into the very structure
of our thought in the use of such words as 'noble' itself, and of its
fourteenth-century synonym, 'gentle'. 'Noble' is applied to a moral
quality, and we are all perfectly well aware that the class of society
that bore the name 'noble' was in moral practice no more noble
than the rest of us. The long tradition of medieval Christian thought
gave to poverty and humility (as we see from Chaucer's *Wife of
Bath's Tale*) the greater praise.

In fact, the peasants, like the Lollard knights, like Chaucer himself in *The Parson's Tale*, were in some ways simply taking seriously,
as laymen, what the Church could be accused of no longer taking

seriously enough, the normal medieval Christian doctrines of the fundamental equality of men, the need for all men to eschew pride and riches, to help their brother Christians, and so forth. These doctrines have always been political dynamite, and well illustrate why the government and the higher clergy were opposed to Lollardy. It threatened to shake the fabric of society. And it is important to say here, since we inherit a nineteenth-century tradition of sympathy for the under-dog and rightful horror at serfdom, that there was much to be said for the government and the higher clergy. First, anarchy itself may create more evils than it has removed; and second, even John Ball, one of the rebel leaders, was not without ambition to rule—he saw himself as future Archbishop of Canterbury—and the peasant leader Wat Tyler was very ready to command. In other words, their Revolt was partly due to personal ambition, and their qualifications for ruling were not as good as those of the then ruling class.

Yet one of the most interesting things about the Revolt was the organising ability of the peasants. There was some loose central organisation, which was different in origin from the widespread local risings, but which fomented them. As so often in revolutions, it may have been that those who provided this centralising force were not simple peasants themselves, but were of higher rank. There was, for example, Thomas Faringdon, a Londoner, neither destitute, a serf, nor illiterate, who travelled about the country as an agitator. The leaders of the Revolt and the chroniclers spoke of a 'Great Society'; the speed with which the Revolt spread, and our knowledge of a few messages, shows that there was some previous organisation and planning; and a letter of John Ball's has survived, half verse, half prose, which looks like a circular.

John Shepherd, some time Saint Mary's priest of York, and now of Colchester, greeteth well John Nameless, and John the Miller, and John Carter, and biddeth them that they be ware of guile in borough, and standeth together in God's name, and biddeth Piers Ploughman go to his work, and chastise Hob the Robber, and taketh with you John Trueman, and all his fellows, and no more, and see you make for your-selves one head, and no more.

> John the Miller hath yground small, small, small;
> The Kingés Son of Heaven shall pay for all.
> Be ware ere ye be woe;
> Knoweth your friend from your foe;
> Haveth enough, and saith 'Ho';
> And do well and better, and fleeth sin;
> And seeketh peace, and hold you there-in;

and so biddeth John Trueman and all his fellows.

The simple piety, the reference to Langland's poem *Piers Plowman*, the commands to seek peace, and to arrange for one leader, are all of importance here. There is a contrast with the risings of the oppressed peasantry of France, who had been worse treated (and whose lot had certainly been made worse by the English invasions), who rose with correspondingly madder violence, and who were put down with greater fury. The English rebels were, at least at first, with a conscious sense of purpose. They attacked not indiscrimin-ately (though there was some paying off of old scores) but went for tax-collectors, lawyers, and Gaunt's men, all of whom were associ-ated with bad government. They burnt archives and court records by which hated rents and the status of serfdom might be proved. When they burnt Gaunt's palace, the Savoy, one story has it that when some looting began they thrust the looters into the flames. They presented a reasoned programme of demands to the King at Mile End (their spokesman probably being Thomas Faringdon), demanding the abolition of serfdom, labour services on a basis of free contract, and the right to rent land at fourpence an acre. In contrast with all this, the government and many persons in authority showed an astonishing failure of nerve. Possibly some of this arose from a half-realised uneasy sense of agreement with the rebels, while the ease with which the rebels entered the great fortress of the Tower suggests that the troops were decidedly in sympathy.

The first spark of rebellion fell in Essex, but the Revolt immediately spread to Kent, to Norfolk and to Suffolk. On Tuesday 11th June 1381, the Kentish men under Wat Tyler, in enormous numbers, left Canterbury to march to Blackheath, just outside London, a seventy-mile journey which they accomplished in the astonishing time of two days. Another great band from Essex arrived at London on 12th June, and encamped at Mile End, in the fields just beyond Aldgate where Chaucer lived. On the 13th the crowd broke into the city, where its original intentions were soon forgotten and violent anarchy reigned. Jack Straw, for example, with a mob, hunted down the Flemings who had been brought in under Edward III to improve the wool-trade. The Flemings' crime was that they were foreigners and workers.

The most vivid account is probably in part at least that of an eye-witness, inserted in *The Anonimalle Chronicle* of York:

> ... the commons took their way to London and did no harm or damage until they came to Fleet Street. There, it was said, the commons of London had set fire to and burned the fair manor of the Savoy before the arrival of the mob from the country.
>
> In Fleet Street the commons from Kent broke open the Fleet Prison and took out all the prisoners and let them go where they would. Then they stopped and pulled down to earth and set fire to a chandler's shop and a blacksmith's shop in the middle of the street, where, it was supposed, there would never be a shop because of spoiling the beauty of the street.
>
> Afterwards they went to the Temple to destroy the tenants of the Temple [i.e. lawyers]; and they pulled down the houses to earth and tore off all the tiles so that they were unroofed and in bad condition. Then they went to the church and took all the books and rolls and records which were in their chests within the Temple of the apprentices of the law and carried them to the great chimney and there burned them.

And in going towards the Savoy they destroyed all the houses which belonged to the Master of the Hospital of St John. Then they went to the palace of the Bishop of Chester, near the church of St Mary-of-the-Strand, where was living Sir John Fordham, bishop-elect of Durham and clerk of the privy seal; and they rolled tuns of wine out of his cellar and drank their fill and so departed without doing more harm.

Then they went to the Savoy and set fire to divers houses of various people . . . on the west. At last they came to the Savoy itself and broke open the gates and entered the place and came to the wardrobe and took all the torches they could find and put them in the fire; and all the cloths and coverlets and beds and hangings of great value, whereof one with heraldic shields was said to be worth a thousand marks [a mark was 13/4—worth sixty times its value today] and all the napery and other goods which they could find they carried into the hall and set fire to them with torches, and they burned the hall and chambers and all the rooms within the gates belonging to the place or manor which the London mob had left without guard. And it was said that they found three barrels of gunpowder, and, thinking it was gold or silver, they threw it into the fire, and it exploded and set the hall on fire and in flame more quickly than the other did, to the great discomfort and damage of the Duke of Lancaster.

The commons of Kent were blamed for the fire, but some said that the London people did it from hatred of the duke. . . .

That same Thursday the mob went to St Martin's-le-Grand and took out of the church, from the High Altar, one Roger Legget, chief tailor, and led him to Cheapside and there beheaded him. That same day eighteen persons were beheaded in different parts of the town. . . .

During this time the King, being in a turret of the great Tower of London, saw the manor of the Savoy and Clerkenwell and the houses of Simon Hosteler by Newgate and the place of John de Butterwyk in flames, and he called all the lords about him into a room and asked their advice as to what should be done in such a crisis. None of them could or would suggest anything; whereupon the young King said he would order the Mayor of the city to command the sheriffs and aldermen to have cried in their wards that everyone between the ages of fifteen and sixty, on pain of life and limb, should be on the morrow at Mile End and meet him there at seven of the bell.[1]

A London account tells how the mob burst into the Tower, dragged out the aged Archbishop Sudbury, who was Lord Chancellor, and several others, and beheaded them on Tower Hill. They carried the heads through the city stuck on lances, and then fixed them, as was always the custom with traitors, on to stakes on London Bridge. It goes on to say,

> Upon the same day there was also no little slaughter within the city, as well of natives as of aliens. Richard Lyons, citizen and vintner of the said city, and many others were beheaded in Cheapside. In the Vintry also there was a very great massacre of Flemings, and in one heap there were lying about forty headless bodies of persons who had been dragged forth from the churches and from their houses; and hardly was there a street in the city in which there were not bodies lying of those who had been slain. Some of the houses also in the said city were pulled down, others in the suburbs destroyed, and others burnt.[2]

The young King met the rebels at Mile End on Friday, and granted their requests. On Saturday, after praying in Westminster Abbey (from which a little earlier the rebels had dragged off a man to slaughter), he met Wat Tyler with a great band of rebels at Smithfield. Wat Tyler presented the usual demands, and included others: that there should be no more lordship save that of the King, all other men to be equal; that the property of the Church should be divided among the laity; and that all but one bishopric should be banished. Perhaps Tyler was insolent; the King's party was nervous; the Mayor, Walworth (one of Chaucer's acquaintances in the customs), lost his temper and pulled down Tyler; a squire finished him off. The peasants set up a great shout of anger, but Richard—it was the great moment of his life, and perhaps only a high-spirited boy of fourteen

---

[1] *The Anonimalle Chronicle*, ed. by V. H. Galbraith; publications of the University of Manchester: Historical Series XLV, 1927, pp. 141-3

[2] H. T. Riley, *Memorials of London and London Life*, II, 1868, pp. 449-51.

could have done it—spurred his horse forward alone to the rebels and cried, 'Sirs, will you shoot your King? I am your captain, follow me.' The rebels knew some discipline and were devoted to the King; they turned and followed him. Walworth rushed back to get some troops, but Richard forbade violence, and ordered the rebels to disperse, contenting himself with replacing Sudbury's head on London Bridge with that of Tyler. Walworth, Brembre, and Philipot (a closer friend of Chaucer's), all great merchants, were knighted for the bold part they played in the insurrection.

The Revolt fizzled out as it was bound to. Society was too hierarchical, the general level of knowledge too low, ideas about government too few, men too unrestrained, for the peasants to be able to maintain it, any more than the government could accept it. Whether it did any real good is impossible to say. At least the poll-taxes were abolished. Perhaps the memory of the Revolt restrained some and encouraged others; but it was severely and rapidly punished, and brought no real improvement in the peasants' situation. Indeed, it is likely that just as the French Revolution hindered reform in this country for forty years, so the Revolt also may have actually hindered social and political progress.

It is possible that one of the bad results of the Revolt was its effect on Richard's character. Son of a loving mother and a stern, irritable, but universally admired father, he was thrust at the age of ten into a position where all, however old, bold, and distinguished, paid at least lip-service to his supremacy. The ancient coronation service had received a few touches emphasising the absolute power of the King, and obscuring the traditional suggestions of election. The almost mystical reverence in which English people hold their sovereign can be illustrated from centuries of English life and literature, but it has never been seen more vividly than in the rebels' behaviour at Smithfield. The success of his own inspired behaviour there, the lamentable failure of old and experienced counsellors, were

The meeting at Mile End and death of Wat Tyler
Radio Times Hulton Picture Library

such as to make a spoilt, high-spirited boy even more wilful and headstrong. Nor was it an age when men easily learnt to control their feelings. It is said that the future Henry IV, when both he and Richard were young men, once in a rage drew his sword on the King himself, within the palace. There are several stories of Richard's uncontrollable wilfulness and inconsistency. Yet he also had a deep emotional need for love and friendship. Indeed his downfall was due not only to his disrespect for the laws and feelings of the English

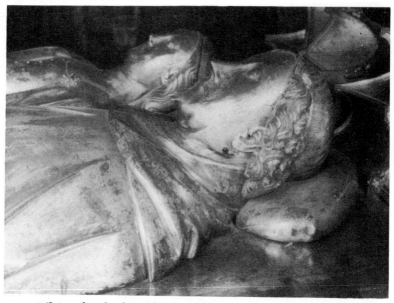

Effigies of Richard II and Anne of Bohemia in Westminster Abbey

people, which his upbringing might account for, but also to his choice of favourites. The chief of these was Aubrey de Vere, distinguished by foolishness and irresponsibility rather than by serious or deliberate wickedness. He was at least loyal to Richard, as many were not, and lost his life for him. When he was killed Richard had his coffin opened and hung for a long time over the corpse, gazing upon its face and fondling the jewelled fingers. He showed the same passion for his wife Anne, whom he married in 1382, when he was fifteen. She was a Bohemian princess, and the marriage was at first one of political convenience—though a chronicler complains that the government paid too much money for such a piece of Eve's flesh. She was plain, as may be seen from the life-like effigy of her made at her death, which now lies in Westminster Abbey. But she was sweet-natured, docile, devout (she had a Bible in English), and Richard was devoted to her. Although chroniclers complain of his late nights, his drinking, his excessive fondness for the company of ladies, he does not seem to have been unfaithful to her. When Anne died in 1393 his grief was so extravagant that he destroyed part of the palace in which she died. When the Earl of Arundel turned up late for the service in Westminster Abbey, and asked permission to withdraw, Richard knocked him to the ground. With Richard's need for affection went an undignified and unrestrained habit of casting insults on all and sundry, and an excessive and humiliating insistence on obsequious behaviour to himself.

The court and the courtiers became increasingly unpopular. They were accused of greed and corruption. The chief of the court party was Sir Simon Burley, the King's tutor. Certainly he made a small fortune for himself, but he was a careerist, in a sense, and all positions round a great man, whether a king or a magnate like Gaunt, were naturally rewarded by a flow of gifts. It would hardly seem that he was in the modern sense of the word corrupt. Practically everybody, including Chaucer, was in the same boat, though men like Chaucer and Burley did a good deal more rowing than those who got the richest pickings, like Aubrey de Vere. Burley was a distinguished man. He was related to the notable scholar Walter Burley, a Merton man (Merton men seem everywhere in the middle of the century), who was tutor of the Black Prince. Simon Burley was born about 1336. He was a man of vigorous and cultivated mind, who owned a number of books. His will of 1388 contains the earliest surviving record in wills of the possession of secular books in English. He was also a distinguished soldier, who accompanied the Black Prince on many of his campaigns, and was much valued by him. This is surely the type of man, intellectually and physically tough, whom we must imagine, in the audience that listened to Chaucer's *Troilus*, attending with as deep an interest to the passages of philosophical poetry on free will, as did others, like the young King and Queen, to the descriptions of love. Burley himself apparently remained unmarried, though Froissart attributes a son to him.

Burley just had time to read or hear Chaucer's *Troilus*, which was completed about 1385-6. The increasing unpopularity of the court with all classes found its leader in the Duke of Gloucester, the youngest and most unpleasant of the King's uncles. In 1386 Gloucester displaced several of the ministers who were associated with the court, and managed to sack a number of the King's men, including Chaucer, who retreated to Kent. For the next couple of years there was a political struggle and then, in 1388, five great lords, who came to be known as the lords appellant, appeared before Parliament in golden surcoats, to challenge Richard's administration. A little before, Richard had shown fight, and Aubrey de Vere had appeared with an army, but he was outgeneralled, and escaped to the Continent. The result of the five lords' appeal was that Richard himself was kept firmly under control, and some of his supporters were executed with varying degrees of shame and severity. Brembre was dragged through the city on a hurdle and hanged, drawn and quartered at Tyburn. So was Tresilian, the Chief Justice. Richard fought hard for Burley, who a contemporary says was a humane man, and with whom many people sympathised. The Queen is said to have gone on her knees to Gloucester to beg him to spare Burley, but to no avail. Burley in view of his service to the royal family, and because he was a Knight of the Garter, was spared the worst shame and pains; on 15th May he was led through the city with his hands bound behind him, and beheaded on Tower Hill. Two other chamber knights suffered similarly, while another suffered the full horrible penalty for treason. Another who suffered the full penalty was Thomas Usk, under-sheriff for Middlesex, connected with Brembre, and also author of *The Testament of Love*. This long prose work is much influenced by Chaucer's translation of *The Consolation of Philosophy*, and by the *Troilus*. In the *Testament* Usk praises Chaucer as 'the noble philosophical poet of love', and it seems likely that Usk was one of a circle, including another chamber knight, Sir John

Clanvowe, which was made up of disciples of Chaucer. Like so many of this circle, he was attracted by Lollardy, but he says that he recanted, and under pressure betrayed his associates. He also seems to have known *Piers Plowman* quite well. Altogether he gives a tantalising glimpse of the city end of Chaucer's literary circle, with its complicated political associations, and one would gladly know more about Thomas Usk. He suffered the full penalty of the law, but was cut down immediately he was hanged, and clumsily beheaded with nearly thirty strokes.

All this was the work of the Merciless Parliament, dominated by the lords appellant. A fortnight later Richard entertained the Parliament at his manor of Kennington, and on 3rd June King, Lords and Commons attended mass in Westminster Abbey, where Richard promised to be 'a good king and lord' for the future, and his subjects renewed their oaths of allegiance. Truly, as Chaucer says in one of his fine moralising lyrics,

> The wrastling for this world axeth a fal.
> Here is non hoom, her nis but wildernesse.

Such was the court and the state of politics which Chaucer knew, and from which he must at this time have withdrawn for a while. It is not surprising that he kept his poetry to personal or to general philosophical or moral themes. Anything of a public nature, apart from flattery (and who could be sure he was flattering the right man?) was clearly impossible. Public themes could only be hinted at even by the obscure Langland. The only type of court poetry on a public theme that could be written was the flattering poem by Chandos Herald already quoted, or such a poem as that in Latin by Richard de Maidstone, celebrating the reconciliation of the King with the Londoners in 1392. It is largely a description of pageantry, which is just the sort of subject that Chaucer usually avoids:

> What nedeth yow rehercen hire array? *tell; their*

he says of the King's feast in *The Squire's Tale*. His courtly audience knew all about these things.

Richard can never have forgotten the bullying he received at the hands of the five lords appellant. It is likely that Gloucester paid for it with his own life in the prison at Calais ten years later. On 3rd May 1389, in full Council, Richard asked his uncle of Gloucester how old he was. Gloucester replied, twenty-two. 'Then,' said Richard, 'I must be old enough to manage my own affairs, as every heir is at liberty to do when he is twenty-one.' For the next six years affairs went tolerably well, with Richard governing with the aid of his Council, and accepting advice and minor restraints. At a Parliament in Stamford in 1392 an admiring foreigner said that never in any realm had he seen a community so noble. But the later years saw an increasing tyranny, and increasing discontent among all sections of the community. Even Richard's policy of reconciliation with the French, which he furthered by his marriage with the seven-year-old princess, increased his unpopularity. Nor had he any military successes of his own, no delight in tournaments, no charm even, with which to win any body of affection to his side. He only indulged his favourites and wasted the enormous capital of affection for the monarch which had been his inheritance. Some have thought that he became mad, or at least unbalanced.

But constitutional history is not everything. For example, from the constitutional and economic points of view, the frequent complaints about the extravagance of the court were perfectly justified; Richard is said to have taken three hundred cooks for his household with him to Ireland. In 1397 the Commons complained about the multitude of bishops and ladies about his court. Yet this extravagance supported a rich court culture, much of it, in the way of feasts and festivals, perishing in the moment of creation; some of it, like the superb remodelling of Westminster Hall, still with us for admiration and use; and some of it, in the way of Latin and French literature, even English literature, still awaiting a full understanding. This 'high culture' is of a kind more associated with French and Italian courts than with English, and we are no doubt right to think it can be bought at too great a price in political, social, and moral stability; but that need not affect its value and interest in itself. Richard, too, was an interesting example of a man both devout and dishonest, but the devotion is as unquestionable as the dishonesty, and not all its seeds need have fallen on stony or thorny or shallow soil. He himself went on pilgrimage to Canterbury; his confessor, Richard Lavenham (a friar), was a man of literary attainments. (One wonders if he and other learned friars were present at the reading of those parts of Chaucer's poetry which are so hostile to the friars.) We shall see something more of this court culture in a later chapter, but it deserves mention here to be held, not in extenuation of Richard's tyranny and mismanagement, especially in the last three years of his reign, but in balance with them. The various aspects of life which in history we inevitably divide are to the living all one. We might take, for example of this and to show that not all Richard's favourites were unworthy, the life of Sir John Montagu. He might not unreasonably have served as a model for Chaucer's Knight, though I am not suggesting that he did.

Sir John was born about 1350, and so was about ten years younger than Chaucer, and also of a nobler family. He received knighthood in 1369, when about the age of Chaucer's Squire, for his bravery in a siege in the French war, when he took two famous French captains prisoner. He had the usual career of war and diplomacy, and in 1391 took part in the celebrated crusade against the Lithuanians, which started from Paris, in which Henry of Derby (later Henry IV) also took part. In the nineties he became closely associated with Richard, and accompanied him to Ireland in 1394. In 1397 he succeeded to his uncle's title and estates as Earl of Salisbury and also to his stall as one of the Knights of the Garter. In the same year Richard

John de Montacute, 3rd Earl of Salisbury, partisan of Richard II
Radio Times Hulton Picture Library

brought about a revenge for the acts of the Merciless Parliament. He caused Parliament to reverse the judgements of the Merciless Parliament, while eight of his lords repeated the role of the five previous lords appellant, accusing three of the previous appellants, the Earls of Gloucester, Arundel, and Warwick, of treason. One of the new appellants, who all appeared in robes of red silk bordered with white and embroidered with gold, was Montagu, the new Earl of Salisbury, who, for his services, received eight of the forfeited manors of Warwick. The next year Salisbury was made Marshal of England, and went to Paris charged with the delicate mission of frustrating the proposed marriage of Henry of Derby with a French princess, in which he succeeded. He accompanied Richard on his last journey to Ireland, and unlike others stood by him loyally when Richard returned to face the invasion of Henry which led to his own capture, deposition and death. Henry himself, when King, seems to have tried to win Salisbury over with merciful treatment, but in January 1400 Salisbury joined in open rebellion with others, and after failing to capture King Henry at Windsor, gathered with troops at Cirencester. There they were surprised and much outnumbered by the townsmen, who killed and beheaded them and sent their heads to Henry. Salisbury had married a rich wife; she was daughter of a London mercer, Adam Fraunceys, the richest man of his day in London, thereby illustrating again the association between court and city, knighthood and trade, which has so marked the upper levels of English life. She had been married twice before, and was twice a widow, most recently of Sir Alan Buxhall, Keeper of the Tower. Salisbury was also distinguished, at any rate in the eighties, as one of the Lollard knights. Chaucer is too elusive to be grouped definitely with this band of important chamber knights, but all the evidence, including that of the Host's contemptuous remarks about Lollardy to the Parson in *The Canterbury Tales*, points to his association with them, who are but the best-known members of the most interesting literary, political, religious, and military movement of the century. Salisbury was at one time a most outspoken Lollard. It was said that when he took over the estate of his wife at Shenley he destroyed all the images of saints that had been set up in the chapel by her two former husbands, except that of St Katherine, which, as it was an object of particular veneration to the people round about, he allowed to be kept in the bake-house. He was also said to attend Lollard services in armour, for their protection. Salisbury, like most of the others of the group, was interested in literature. He had a name for writing poetry in French, of which, unfortunately, none has so far been traced. And he commissioned the French chronicle of the last days of Richard II which was written by a French gentleman called Creton, who travelled with Salisbury and Richard on the last journeys in Ireland and Wales. Creton says of Salisbury,

I sincerely loved him, because he heartily loved the French: and besides he was humble, gentle, and courteous in all his doings, and he had everyone's word for being loyal and prudent in all places. He gave most largely, and his gifts were profitable. Bold he was, and courageous as a lion. Right well and beautifully did he also make ballads, songs, roundels and lays. Though he was but a layman, so gracious were all his deeds, that never, I think, shall that man issue from his country in whom God hath implanted so much worth as was in him.[1]

The famous French poetess, Christine de Pisane, knew him and called him 'a gracious knight, loving poems, and himself a gracious poet'. He was a friend of Christine's and began to educate her son, aged thirteen, in his household, after the fashion of those times. The son came to England in 1398, and after Salisbury's death, Henry IV, who also admired Christine's poems, wished to retain her son under his protection, and to entice Christine to come and adorn his court as she did the French. But she had too low a view of the faith of the English, especially after the death of Richard and Salisbury, so she held off until she got her son back, and finally did not come.

Such were the life and attainments of Sir John Montagu, third Earl of Salisbury, and a representative, if outstanding, member of the court of Richard. He, like Burley, Clanvowe, and others, including Richard himself and Anne his wife, are the audience we must assume for Chaucer's poetry, and the persons whom we must assume as part of his normal life and activity. Chaucer himself must have been somewhat of their type, except that whereas they were knights, he was a man of books. But all were men of affairs, and of the same kind of affairs. Chaucer took part in diplomatic missions with these men, and served on government commissions with them. When Richard asserted his own capacity to rule, in 1389, he put back a number of his own men in the government, and Chaucer was eventually one of these. Chaucer became Clerk of the Works, a position that had been held in the past by such important men in the government as Bishop William Wykeham. When in 1390 the

[1] French Metrical History of Richard II, trans. by Webb, Archaeologia XX.

great jousts were held at Smithfield, which are described in detail by Froissart, it was Chaucer's responsibility to have the scaffolding erected. When he relinquished the Clerkship in 1391 he was given what was probably the sinecure of a subforestership. It cannot be said that he was very richly patronised, considering his fame as a poet, but he received a number of small grants and pensions, although he was also short of money. He also received some presents from Gaunt's son Henry of Derby. He was becoming elderly, so that it is possible that in the nineties he was withdrawing from active court life. In the personal poem to Scogan, which begins humorously, and which must have been written in the nineties, he says he has given up poetry; it rusts in the sheath in peace. He asks Scogan to cause him to be remembered at the 'stream's head of grace, honour, and worthiness', by which he presumably means the court, saying that he himself is at the end of that stream 'forgotten in solitary wilderness'. There is no sign that he was ever a close personal follower of Richard. The old courtier, however, drew his Muse from the sheath once more at the end of the reign, of the century, and of his own life, when, on Henry's accession, he wrote a witty poem about the lightness of his purse, in which he echoes the formula used to justify Henry's usurpation of the throne. Like all sensible men he accepted the new ruler, and it is pleasant to know that Henry immediately granted Chaucer a new pension and also confirmed his former grants from Richard. This was in 1399. In 1400 Chaucer died.

CHAPTER FOUR

At Home

PUBLIC life, however exciting, is built on the foundation of the private life, the life of men at home, in their family relationships, manners, houses, food, and clothing. At home means being with the family. Hardly anyone lived alone in the fourteenth century, except possibly the recluse or hermit, who did so for religious reasons. Even these were less solitary than one might think. There was a celebrated recluse at Westminster Abbey who cannot have been much out of the way, for he was celebrated for political wisdom and even the King occasionally consulted him. Langland says that

> Hermits in a heap, with hooked staves,
> Went to Walsyngham, and their wenches after.

There can have been few lonely housewives; the aged (in so far as there were any) would normally live with their children; and for the really destitute there were many 'hospitals', that is, almshouses, founded by the devout. That is not to say that life was anything like as comfortable or as pleasant as it is today. Not only were the vast majority terribly poor, but their life was extremely insecure. A rainy summer could bring them to starvation; there was far more violence and no police force, far more risk of accident and fire and no insurance, far more disease and no scientific medicine, no nurses, no hospitals in the modern sense, few doctors and those expensive. These were the natural and accepted conditions of life and they made it all the more necessary to band together. Of all the many ways in which people banded together the family was both the most important and the general model. The core of the family is of course father, mother, and children, and in our days this is *the* family. But even in Victorian times the natural family often contained more than this, with a grandparent or two, or a maiden aunt. Many such families also had servants. In the fourteenth century such servants were a part, though an inferior part, of the family itself. If the father were a great lord his 'family' (Latin *familia*) was enormous. He had a council of men of wealth and standing, some of whom lived with him, with their wives, who acted as waiting-women to the lord's lady, and whose children grew up with the lord's children. He had secretaries, chaplains, a master-at-arms, besides servants of all kinds—personal servants, waiting-men, grooms, kennelmen, huntsmen, and the rest. The King himself was only the greatest lord among many such, yet he was felt to be in some sense 'the father of his people'. A priest was a 'father' and the Pope the 'Holy Father'. In cities the merchants carried on business in their own houses, apprentices were fed and clothed by their masters, fed at their table, regulated like sons and daughters, and punished as heartily. The peasants, especially if bondmen, were held with something like the same close tie to their lords.

There were in many respects fewer real differences between the rich and all but the desperately poor than we should perhaps expect. Take for instance the sizes of families. With a few notable exceptions (like Edward III) the usual size of the 'natural' family seems to have been small at all levels of society. This is not because few children were born, but because many died. Until the middle of the nineteenth century in England about three-quarters of all children born died before they were six. Even after six it was very easy to die of what is now a simple accident, like breaking a leg or an arm. Men were old at sixty, which was about the age at which Chaucer died, and in one of his late poems he complains how age 'dulls' his spirit. It has been calculated that in the seventeenth century half the population was under sixteen years old; the proportion must have been much the same in the fourteenth. We can hardly imagine how people were continually surrounded with death, how insecure they felt, and how ready they must have been, to support life at all, to seize the joy of the passing moment.

Much of this we can work out from the records of the times, but also, in more immediate human terms, from the poetry of Chaucer. The father was very much the head of the family, the pivot on whom all turned, for if he died the family was thrown into poverty. The father was often rather remote, for his concern was with the world of work, and he didn't change nappies or help with the housework. He was loved, and feared. Bartholomew notes that a father will give up his own food for his child, but also shows his children 'no glad cheer' lest they be proud. The sort of words that go with 'father' in Chaucer's writing shows us the typical father. He is called 'old' six times, 'wise' and 'dear' three. Then once or twice each he is called 'good', 'benign', 'ready', 'free' (meaning generous or noble), but also 'woeful', 'poor', 'hoary', 'stern', 'hard', 'wretched', 'jealous', 'false', 'cruel'. A father is clearly a formidable person, who is capable of arousing resentment as well as love and respect. Contrast these words with those that are used with the word 'mother'. A mother is never old, hoary, false, jealous, hard, stern, cruel; nor good, wise, ready. But she is called 'dear' fourteen times, and once or twice 'free', 'meek', 'kind', 'sweet', 'blissful', 'woeful'. A mother is a kinder, softer, sweeter person, more loved and less respected, who also has a scrap of joy that the father misses. The word most often used for children is 'little', and in so far as Chaucer's poetry deals with children he shows a most tender, indeed almost sentimental, affection for them, especially for babies. Langland, indeed, blamed parents for being too indulgent to children whom they feared to lose by sickness. Although the English have for centuries been remarked by foreigners for their harshness to children and sentimentality towards animals, family affection seems to have been strong in Chaucer's England. There was certainly sentimentality towards animals, too, if Chaucer's Prioress was at all typical. She wept if she saw a mouse caught in a trap, and kept pet dogs, which she fed on the finest food, and over which she wept if one were struck, or died. Chaucer shows no sign of sharing this sentimentality.

What is perhaps odd to us is the way people could shrug off deep and genuine feeling and quickly turn to joy and joking. If they felt more passionately than we do, they also felt less persistently. I have quoted the general French opinion of English 'fickleness', which is chiefly a political judgement, and which Englishmen might well call their good sense and refusal to bear tyranny, even from an anointed king. Those who have accused us of fickleness have not kept their monarchy and their ancient laws as long as we have. But part of this fickleness may also have been the changeable emotions of a less sophisticated people. The English reputation for calmness does not begin till the eighteenth century. It is very noticeable how ready to weep Englishmen were in the fourteenth century, how they tended to fling themselves about when in a rage. Henry of Lancaster says that when he was angry he was out of sense and reason, would hit people with fist and knife, sword and stick, kick people, tear his own and other people's hair and clothes; while on the other hand, when in friendly mood, he would hug his friends round their necks. The tendency to weep and wail is apt to make us feel that Chaucer's hero, Troilus, is something of a milksop; yet he is called the greatest warrior in Troy after Hector himself. Fourteenth-century Englishmen had the emotionalism which in modern times the English attribute to the French, and much the same habits of kissing. Such ready emotionalism brought joy and sorrow much closer together—as Chaucer says

And also joie is next the fyn of sorwe. *end*

Troilus I, l. 952

Chaucer, time and again, puts side by side the perfectly serious and

71

the humorous or cynical, so that we may either, with our less quick-silver feelings, feel that he spoils the effect of the one with the other, or we may wrongly assume that only one effect, either serious or humorous, is truly meant. Again, Chaucer surprises us with the flippancy or cynicism with which he can comment on something he normally treats seriously. Although he shows himself very tender to the sweetness and helplessness of little children, and although there is no poet who more often expresses sympathy and pity for ladies in distress, he can say, of an amusing but highly improper incident,

> And up he yaf a roryng and a cry, *gave*
> As dooth the mooder whan the child shal dye.
>
> *The Merchant's Tale, C.T.* IV, ll. 2364-5

We know practically nothing about Chaucer's family life. There are no records of his childhood, because the interest in biography, as we know it, had yet to be born. We may guess that Chaucer had a fond mother and a loving, though stern, father, because that was precisely what most people had. A good example of the pattern was Edward III, though he was unusual in having such a large family of children, for he had four sons and three daughters who grew up, as well as several more who died young. The royal family feeling was strong, and his Queen, Philippa, was notably good, gracious, kind, and loyal to Edward.

Something here should be said about marriage, though one must remember that the vast number of ordinarily happy or ordinarily unhappy marriages, then as now, escaped notice because of their ordinariness. We tend to hear most about the unusual. On the other hand, what is outstanding, and therefore unusual, is often, paradoxically, what is most characteristic of an age. The forms of the unusual magnify what is normal, and the unusual varies from age to age, in a continuous society like that of England, more than the normal does. Men married for the usual variety of reasons; because they were in love, as the Black Prince married Joan of Kent, and as his brother married Blanche of Lancaster, whose early death Chaucer wrote about in *The Book of the Duchess*. They also married for land and money (and the two princes are examples of this too). And no doubt many married then as now because they wanted to be married and to have children and they married whom they could get. Many marriages were arranged by parents or friends and sometimes girls in especial were forced into marriage with men they didn't like. In the highest circles mere children were sometimes married; Edward's son Lionel was 'married' at the age of four, to a wealthy heiress, for obvious reasons. Richard II's second wife, the French princess Isabella, whom he married in 1396 for reasons of state, was then seven years old. On the other hand, though men might often marry in their early 'teens, as did Richard his first wife, or Edward III, the records show many men marrying late. (This may sometimes be because the record of an earlier marriage has been lost, for until the twentieth century women were in general less long-lived than men. Women's 'weakness' was partly due to their lives being restricted to damp and draughty houses, whereas men lived more active outdoor lives, but it was perhaps due more to continuous childbearing, and no doubt to the emotional strain of seeing child after child sickly and dying.) Sir Richard Stury is not known to have married until he was about fifty. Sir Lewis Clifford married about forty. But a more usual age was the early twenties, when Chaucer himself married. Women were usually younger. The miller's daughter in *The Reeve's Tale* remained unmarried at twenty, but there are indications that she felt this to be a little late.

How moral people were is difficult to judge, especially as our own standards in these matters have changed so rapidly in the last twenty years. Probably the highest and lowest ranks of society have always been less moral than the middling ranks. In a village a girl who had a baby before she was married had to pay a fine called a *leyrwite*, but immorality was widespread among serfs and even the poor clergy. At the other end of the scale Edward III had his mistress, Alice Perrers, when he fell into dotage. She was much hated, for political rather than moral reasons. The Black Prince married for love, when he was thirty and Joan thirty-two, but had an illegitimate son, Sir Roger de Clarendon. Gaunt's second marriage was a political one, and he lived for many years with the governess of his children, Katherine Swinford, who was Chaucer's sister-in-law. When his second wife died he married Katherine (much to the annoyance of the ladies of the court, who considered her rank inferior) and had his children by her made legitimate. Henry of Lancaster says his worst sins were sloth and lechery, but especially lechery. He would rather talk to or kiss an immoral woman, he says, than a moral one, and he often enticed some foolish lady to lechery. On the whole people seem not to have worried very much about illegitimacy, though it was not of course approved of. The Church was in theory a bulwark of morality, although there are plenty of instances of priests living with women. Even in such a case, however, we must remember the earlier tradition of married priests; the long battle which forced celibacy upon the clergy in the eleventh century was never entirely won. Even what was sin to the fourteenth century may have been practised with love and constancy. There must also have been chaste and holy lives in the Church, just as there must have been many faithful husbands and wives. Where Chaucer stands in this it is impossible to say. For all the cynicism and worldliness of some of his poetry it is fundamentally moral. He was married, and had perhaps two sons. At the same time there is the uncomfortable fact that he was accused of rape. Rape may have meant abduction for the purpose of marrying the woman off to somebody else for reasons of profit (such an attempt was made on Chaucer's own father when he was only eleven, by an aunt) but it may have meant rape in the modern sense. The emotional as well as the physical violence of the age comes out here, though it was not an age so much obsessed with sex as our own, at least as far as literature is concerned.

One of the notable characteristics of the age, at least in literature, and among the upper classes, was the association of love with marriage. In contrast with French literature love affairs are normally expected to lead to marriage. Chaucer is a partial exception, since he treats humorously of illicit love. Men, or at least courtiers, often combined the expression of love with profitable marriage, and it is typical of Richard that even when his affairs were at their worst he thought tenderly of his child-wife and spoke of her in the language of love as '*m'amie*', '*ma compaigne*'.

Love itself was not necessarily associated either with sexual experience or with marriage, and was the subject of an enormous literature and of a whole set of conventions of behaviour, which I shall discuss later. Like most personal relationships at that period it was thought of not in terms of companionship but in terms of superiors and inferiors. In love it was the lady who was superior. This made for some awkwardness, for after marriage the position was completely reversed. A wife was completely subordinate to her husband, and had no right to property or to anything else, even to her children. Wife beating was common. An extreme example of this subordination of the wife to the husband is given by the favourite medieval tale of Patient Griselda, who meekly endured terrible sufferings inflicted on her by her husband to prove her patience and loyalty. It was told by Boccaccio and Petrarch, and Chaucer tells the story in *The Clerk's Tale*. But he finishes up with a cynical ending, recommending wives on no account to follow Griselda's example. Chaucer, almost alone of great English writers till the nineteenth century, deals at some length with marriage relations, and one of his greatest creations, satirical but also sympathetic, is the much-married Wife of Bath, who tyrannised over all her successive husbands, and made their lives a misery. His solution to the problem of a successful marriage is given at the beginning of *The Franklin's Tale*, where the knightly husband promises always to obey his wife 'as any lover to his lady shall', but 'for shame of his degree' will retain the 'name of sovereignty', that is, shall be master before the world. She, on the other hand, promises always to be his 'humble true wife'. Humility was a great virtue in fourteenth-century England.

An authoritarian pattern of family life was perhaps the more necessary because houses were so crowded and there was so little privacy for anyone. Troilus was a great prince, and lived in a palace very probably thought of as being like one of the great nobles' houses on the Strand. But the only place he can be private in is his own bedroom, and Pandarus finds it easy to intrude on him even there. There was a wealthy merchant in the fifteenth century who had a wife and seven children, but had only one bedroom, though the enormously rich Richard Lyons had no less than four bedrooms. He was unusual in many ways. Even the squires of the King's household were expected to sleep two to a bed. At the other end of the scale a peasant's cottage would have only one room, sometimes shared with animals, or perhaps two, a 'hall' where all lived, and a bower, or bedroom, separated from the hall by a partition and all under one roof. In most cases the whole family must have slept in one bed, or on one heap of bedding. Chaucer describes very vividly how a poor widow lived with her two daughters in such a 'narrow cottage':

> Thre large sowes hadde she, and namo   *no more*
> Three keen, and eek a sheep that highte Malle,   *cows; was called*
> Ful sooty was hire bour and eek her halle,   *bower*
> In which she eet ful many a sklendre meel.
> Of poynaunt sauce hir neded never a deel.   *spicy*
> No deyntee morsel passed thurgh hir throte....
> No wyn ne drank she, neither whit ne reed;

Hir bord was served moost with whit and blak
Milk and broun breed, in which she foond no lak,
Seynd bacoun, and somtyme an ey or tweye. *grilled; egg; two*
    The Nun's Priest's Tale, C.T. VII, ll. 2830-45

She also had a fenced garden for the hens to run in, and in the garden
a bed of green vegetables, where later a fox lay hid. She did not
live in a solitary place, for when the fox ran off with the cock there
chased after him not only the widow and her two daughters but
other men, and dogs, and 'Malkyn with a distaff in her hand'. There
is a busy little community implied here, poor, but not desperate.
There is another glimpse of decent poverty in *The Clerk's Tale* which
vividly shows both the physical details and the ideal beauty of proper
behaviour. Griselda's house stood near the palace in a village which
was in a delightful position. The poorest of the villagers was Jani-
cula, the father of Griselda:

But for to speke of vertuous beautee,
Thanne was she oon the faireste under sonne;   *one (of)*
For povreliche yfostred up was she,   *poorly; bred*
No likerous lust was thurgh hire herte yronne.   *lecherous*
Wel ofter of the welle than of the tonne   *wine-cask*
She drank, and for she wolde vertu plese,
She knew wel labour, but noon ydel ese.

But thogh this mayde tendre were of age,
Yet in the brest of hire virginitee
Ther was enclosed rype and sad corage; *a mature and constant heart*
And in greet reverence and charitee
Hir olde povre fader fostred shee.   *cherished*
A fewe sheep, spynnynge, on feeld she kepte; *while she was spinning*
She wolde noght been ydel til she slepte.

And whan she homward cam, she wolde brynge
Wortes, or other herbes tymes ofte,   *vegetables*

The whiche she shredde and seeth for hir lyvynge,   *boiled*
And made hir bed ful hard and nothyng softe.

The Clerk's Tale, C.T. IV, ll. 211-28

It was when she was carrying a pot of water from the well that the Marquis, who became her husband, first met her.

Though Chaucer saw that poverty was painful, he also thought, in common with men of his age, and in sharp contrast with ours, that there was no shame in poverty, and that when bravely borne it had more moral virtue than other lives. 'Glad poverte is an honest [*honourable*] thing,' says the Wife of Bath in her tale, and devotes a large part of it to showing that true nobility comes from virtue, not from rank or riches. 'Fy on possessioun [*riches*],' says the Franklin in *The Canterbury Tales*, 'but if a man be vertuous withal.' Men could believe this as well as believe that 'magnificence' (what we should call 'conspicuous consumption') was the proper virtue of kings and princes. Chaucer has respect for poverty and does not sentimentalise it, but there is no note in his writings, as there is especially in the religious writers of the age, of deep sympathy for the hard life of the poor. For this we must turn to Langland, in a famous passage:

The most needy are our neighbours, if we take good heed,
As prisoners in pits, and poor folk in cottages
Charged with children, and chief-lords' rent,
What they with spinning may spare, spend it in house-hire,
Both in milk and in meal, to make with porridge,
To glut with their children, that cry after food.
Also themselves suffer much hunger,
And woe in winter-time, with waking at nights,
To rise to the narrow room, to rock the cradle,
Both to card and to comb, to patch and to wash,
To rub and to reel, rushes to peel,
That ruth is to read of, or in rhyme show,
The woe of these women, that dwell in cottages,

And of many other men, that much woe suffer.

They are ashamed to beg, and have nothing but their jobs, poorly paid, to enable them to feed their children.

> There is bread and penny-ale, as for a pittance taken,
> Cold flesh and cold fish, instead of baked venison;
> Fridays and fasting-days a farthing's-worth of mussels
> Were a feast for such folk, or so many cockles.
>> *Piers Plowman*, C X, ll. 71 ff.

Langland's great poem is full of details of the life of the poor, with which there is little to compare in Chaucer.

When we turn to the houses and home-life of other grades of society, there is more variety and more comfort, though not much more privacy. The miller was an important man in the village, and better off than most. There is an amusing sketch of one called Simkin in *The Reeve's Tale*. He had married the local parson's illegitimate daughter, and she had brought 'full many a pan of brass' with her as a dowry. For village folk they were well off, but Simkin seems to have had only two rooms in his house, one the general living and eating room, the other the bedroom he shared with his wife, they sleeping in a double bed, with his twenty-year-old daughter in her own bed, and the six-month-old baby in the cradle. In the room he put up another spare bed for the two university students to share. He himself wore a white nightcap, and possibly a nightshirt, but it is probable that most people slept naked.

Since Chaucer's father was a rich merchant in London he presumably had a fairly large house. There is a record of a house that was built for a merchant next to the Customs Wharf, where Chaucer was Controller. It was to be of three storeys, the first twelve feet, the second ten feet, the third seven feet high. There was to be a hall forty feet long and twenty-four feet broad, and a parlour, kitchen, and buttery, all built on cellars seven feet deep. The rest of the site

Above The fourteenth-century house in Chipping Campden, Gloucestershire, of William Grevel, one of the greatest wool-merchants   *Crown Copyright*

Below Fourteenth-century weavers' houses (with later windows). Flemish weavers' houses, Lavenham, Suffolk   *Crown Copyright*

was to be used for chambers and houses for merchandise, for the merchant carried out his business on the premises. All building was to be in new wood, except presumably the cellars, which would be of stone. More details from the same house in the fifteenth century, when it came to be known as Browne's Place, show that it had many small rooms, a chapel, a counting-house, inside lavatories, one at least with running water, and a courtyard, probably with a small garden. This was an unusually splendid house, but the main features, including the garden, where vegetables, herbs, spices, and flowers might be grown, were found in many houses. The same kind of house is owned by the rich merchant in *The Shipman's Tale*; it has a garden, presumably a private chapel, since they can arrange to say Mass when they please, a counting-house on the premises where the merchant does his work, and a kitchen with several cooks. The wife of such a rich man has no work to do, and seems to have a very free time, an impression that the Wife of Bath also gives, though she is supposed, in the *General Prologue*, to have a business of her own.

For some time Chaucer occupied the rooms above the city gate at Aldgate, but unluckily we know little of their arrangement. There was a garden and a cellar; the great double gate occupied the ground-floor space, and perhaps the gate-warden had a room or two at the side of the gate. The great gate was supposed to be shut at sunset, and the wicket at curfew. Then the noise of passers-by and the rumble of heavy carts would stop at last. It seems to have been a sought-after residence, pleasant for its nearness to the fields, and convenient for the city and for Chaucer's place of work at the Customs Wharf.

The great houses of the nobility and the great churchmen, even the King's palaces themselves, in so far as they were not fortresses, were probably not so very different from such houses as Browne's Place. They were scattered about the town, or along the Strand, and were not gathered in one area, as they would be in modern

England. There were no 'one-class' suburbs. Rich and poor rubbed shoulders, beggars gathered outside the gates, and fed on the crumbs from the rich man's table. Inside the gates were the courtyard, the hall, kitchen etc., some rooms, including one mainly for ladies, called the solar, and perhaps the garden behind. Criseyde's house is variously called a palace, a house, a place. It is in a street a little way off from the city proper, and is perhaps imagined as being in some such situation as in the Strand, though it is within the city walls. Downstairs it has a hall and a paved parlour; upstairs it has Criseyde's bedroom which has a cedar tree just outside the window, a living room with a bay window, and another smaller room. Possibly the windows were glazed, though that would have been very expensive. Chaucer, in *The Book of the Duchess*, relates that he dreamt he awoke in a bedroom of which the windows were glazed with stained glass on which was shown the whole story of Troy. Such windows are cheaper in poetry than in life, but certainly the Black Prince paid a glazier to put in medallions of stained glass in the windows of one of his houses. In Criseyde's house the garden was reached by steps down from one of the ground-floor rooms, but we are told only that it had shaded sanded walks, with new benches.

The lighting of houses was always a problem. The peasants' cottages were smoky and dark, by day lit by the door and a little window which was either unglazed or covered by oiled paper which did not let much light through. At night the fire in the middle of the hall, used for simple cooking and for warmth, gave a glimmer, but candles were expensive:

... glowing embers gladdeth not these workmen
That work and wait in winters nights,
As doth a candle that hath caught fire and blazeth.
Piers Plowman, C XX, ll. 183-5

If a man were rich enough he might have his windows large and glazed. John of Gaunt's great new hall at Kenilworth Castle, of which the ruins may still be seen, shows the latest trends, for the windows are large and beautiful and must have been filled with glass; there is no thought of and no possibility of defence. At night, light was provided by tallow and wax candles of various sizes, and in ordinary households these were usually made at home, like so much else for daily consumption. The squires and valets of the King's household, of whom Chaucer was one, drew as part of their daily pay and rations in winter time two Paris (i.e. tallow) candles and a supply of firewood. In halls there were burning torches which once or twice offer Chaucer an image of brightness, but one would have thought they were flaring and smoky at the best. Churches also were often dark, though there was a strong tendency to larger windows, as there was in secular architecture. It is no wonder that, other reasons apart, people thought of heaven as a blaze of light. In the country, unless people had to work, they probably went to bed at dusk. Even Chaucer says, in *The Parliament of Fowls*, that when daylight faded he stopped reading and went to bed. But in *The Book of the Duchess* he tells us how he read in bed at night, because he couldn't sleep, and a lord would have a nightlight all night. In *The Squire's Tale* a court festivity goes on till nearly dawn, and in Simkin's house, the mill in *The Reeve's Tale*, they sit up drinking and talking by the fire till midnight. In a mainly wooden city, with so many naked lights, there was the constant danger of fire, which culminated in the seventeenth-century Great Fire of London, which destroyed so much of medieval London. Perhaps the popular representation of the terrors of hell as the torment of flames drew much of its force from this ever-present fear.

At whatever time people went to bed, they usually got up earlier than most of us do now. Chaucer says of the festivity described in *The Squire's Tale* that the revellers did not get up till prime, which was nine o'clock in the morning, and this is felt to be unusually late. The King's daughter in this tale, the beautiful Canacee, was much more sensible, and went to bed early, and got up at dawn, though her old governess asked why she was up so early. Canacee made her waiting women all get up and go for a walk with her. One imagines they were not pleased, but to tell us that sort of detail was not the poet's aim. Richard arranged to meet the rebels at Mile End at 7 a.m. In the city the gates were supposed to be opened at dawn, and in *The Nun's Priest's Tale* a corpse is taken out of the city at dawn in a dung-cart. All of which means that labouring men and farmers got up earlier and worked harder than others, as they do now. But the merchant in *The Shipman's Tale* got up early too, and had done a good deal of his day's work by prime, while his wife walked up and down in the garden impatiently waiting for break-fast, as we should call it, but which they called dinner, a meal they took after quickly hearing Mass. Presumably they had a bite to eat when they first got up. Coffee and tea were unknown; when he first got up the Franklin used to have a 'sop in wine', which was a sauce of wine, almond milk, saffron, ginger, sugar, cinnamon, cloves, and mace, poured over the best white bread. He did himself rather unusually well.

As the portrait of the Franklin suggests, food became increasingly luxurious and elaborately prepared in the fourteenth century. The word *feast* meant originally a religious festival, and in so far as it was opposed to a fast it always implied eating. But it is first in the four-teenth century that the word came to be used in the deliberately limited sense of 'a splendid meal'. Even the rich, however, were much more at the mercy of seasons and harvests than we have been for many years. There was no importation of foodstuffs except spices, and no means of preserving foods except by salt and spices. Scarcity is itself a value, and we can hardly imagine the relish there must have been for fresh meat after a long cold winter, towards the end of which there was little except old salt-pickled meat to eat in all but the greatest houses. In the summer and autumn the amount of meat consumed at a meal by those who could buy it seems appalling, but they made up for it with almost necessary Lenten fasting, while the poor were mostly vegetarian in their diet.

The standard food for a farm labourer was cheese and oaten cakes, though Langland complains that after a good harvest labourers refused cheap bacon and day-old cabbage, demanding new corn, wheat bread, fresh meat, and fish. Oysters and cockles were thought poor stuff. At other times, the poor had to manage without meat, though Chaucer's poor widow had her bacon.

> I have no penny, said Piers, pullets to buy,
> Nor geese nor pigs, but two green cheeses,
> And a few curds and cream, and unleavened cake,
> And a loaf of beans and bran, baked for my children.
> And I say, by my soul, I have no salt bacon,
> Nor no cocks' eggs, by Christ, collops to make,
> But I have onions and parsley and many cabbages,
> And also a cow and a calf.
>
> *Piers Plowman*, A VII, ll. 267-74

But Piers had a half-acre of his own; serfs and landless men were not so well off, and knew well the sound of their children crying for hunger. The usual drink for all ages was ale made at home without hops, though water was also there for pious females.

Diet among the poor and middling classes in the towns was not so very different, save that in a place like London there was more chance of variety, of spices, perhaps less chance of picking up a rabbit, and certainly less chance of poaching the king's deer, or of getting the leavings from a great man's hunting of deer or boars. All houses except those of the poor had vegetable gardens and often a few fruit tress, and many people in the town kept pigs.

When we come to consider the meals of the rich, the difference is not only one of food. Eating becomes part of the art of life. A fantastic variety of flesh, fish, and fowl was consumed, including much for which we should have little taste, like the tough and fishy swan. There was also a great variety of tasty ingredients, such as those already mentioned in connection with the Franklin's 'sop in wine'. Erasmus over a century later considered that the English had too great a taste for sauces, and the modern word 'saucepan' for a general cooking pot is significant. The 'poudre-marchant tart' that Chaucer's Cook knew so well how to provide contained among other things powdered ginger, cinnamon, and galingale, which last was an aromatic East Indian root. The whole could have wine added to give the sharpness that was so much desired—woe was the Franklin's cook but if his sauce was poignant and sharp. It was not merely jaded palates that demanded such stimulation; conditions of storage were such that it must often have been necessary to disguise, rather than enhance, the taste of the basic food. This was surely the function of mustard. And although there were by-laws against it Chaucer's Cook was not likely to be the only one who served up old pies in his shop as if they were fresh.

At feasts huge quantities were consumed. Dr G. C. Coulton calculated that at a funeral feast for a bishop each person managed a pound and three-quarters of bread, one two-hundredth of an ox, one sixtieth of a hog, one thirtieth of a sheep, one sixth of a goose, five and a half pints of ale, three and a half pints of wine, and oddments of poultry, etc. Of course animals were smaller then than now—but a pint wasn't!

A whole elaborate ceremonial went to the serving up of food in a great man's house. In the early fifteenth century there began a series of 'books of nurture' (or 'courtesy'), in English, which teach the ceremonial involved, as well as giving many instructions for the education and good behaviour of the young. One of the earliest and best of these is John Russell's *Book of Nurture*. Russell describes himself as usher and marshal of Humphrey, Duke of Gloucester, and wrote probably in the second quarter of the fifteenth century, copying

Coconut drinking-cup

from and elaborating earlier writings of the same kind in French and Latin.

Give to your sovereign fresh bread, he says, to others one-day-old bread, to the household three-day-old bread; and for trenchers (that is, the slices of bread that were used as side-plates) use four-day bread. Make sure that cutlery and table-cloths are clean. Serve fruit in season, figs, raisins, almonds, dates also, butter, cheese, nuts, apples and pears, fruit-preserves, jams, quince-marmalade, white and green ginger (ginger is very frequently mentioned in recipes). Before dinner (the first main meal of the day) serve plums, damsons, cherries, grapes; after dinner serve pears, nuts, strawberries, whinberries, and hard cheese, also white apples and pippins, or caraway seed in jam. After supper (the last of the two main meals of the day) serve roasted apples, pears, 'blanch powder' (a powder of ginger, cinnamon and nutmeg) 'your stomach for to ease'. He comments on the various powers of these foods to bind and to loose, and says beware of salads, green foods, and raw fruit, for these make many a man to have a feeble belly. And indeed, though this may go against modern views, when one remembers the ignorance of microbes, and the primitive sanitation of the times, this seems good advice, just as it is good advice in the Far East, very often, today. Lettuces were eaten boiled—when so treated they come out rather like inferior cooked spinach. But a raw apple will cure indigestion, he says, from various drinks, and 'measure [moderation] is a merry mean'. Then there are instructions for setting the table; all diners are to have knife, spoon, and napkin (fingers were made before forks, which did not come into general use until the sixteenth century). There follow directions as to behaviour when serving the guests; don't scratch, wriggle, fiddle with yourself, pick your nose, retch, or spit too far (!) or laugh too loud, or lick the dish to clean it; the very need to mention things of this sort makes one shudder. Much time is spent on instructions how to carve various kinds of flesh and fowl, and then there is advice on what is and is not indigestible. Then we come to some truly staggering menus which bring home to us just what it meant that in the Franklin's house it 'snowed of meat and drink'. The three-course dinner of flesh will serve as an example.

First mustard and brawn are put out, and soup of herbs, spice, and wine; then beef, mutton, stewed pheasant, swan, with 'chawdwyn' (made of chopped liver and entrails boiled with blood, bread, wine vinegar, pepper, cloves and ginger); these further accompanied with capon, pig, baked venison, meat fritter, and a 'leche lombard'. This latter was something similar to the 'chawdwyn' only more so, of so hectic a richness that 'the sense faints picturing it'. That is the first course, and it is followed by a 'subtlety', which was an elaborate table-decoration figuring a scene or action of some kind. In the present menu it is a device of the Salutation, Gabriel greeting Mary with an Ave.

Then follows the second course. First two soups, 'blank manger' (which is one of the dishes Chaucer's Cook makes so well, basically a mish-mash of white meats like chicken sweetened and spiced etc.), and also jelly. Then roast venison, kid, fawn or rabbit (here for the first time we seem to be given alternatives), bustard, stork, crane, peacock (sown back in its skin when cold after roasting), young heron or bittern, to be served with bread if there is anything to drink. There follows partridge, woodcock, plover, egret, sucking rabbits, larks, sea-bream, sweet cakes, puff pastry, with another 'leche', amber jelly, and poached fritter; and a subtlety to complete the course of an angel singing with merry cheer to three shepherds on a hill.

The third course begins with almond cream, 'mawmeny' (well-spiced chicken's brawn), curlew, snipes, quails, sparrows, roast martins, perch (a fish) in jelly, freshwater crayfish, fish pies, baked quinces, another kind of 'leche', a fritter, and a ceremonious subtlety of the Three Wise Men giving presents to the Mother of Christ.

After this comes the dessert of white apples, caraway, wafers, with ypocras to drink. Then those who are able to stagger away, we may think, are free to do so.

It would be only a burden to go through in the same detail the equally splendid dinner of fish. Instead I shall quote the account of a feast in another great poem, written in Chaucer's lifetime somewhere in the north-west midlands, *Sir Gawain and the Green Knight*. It is just as courtly, devout, and sophisticated as the poetry of Chaucer, though in a different idiom, which I modernise slightly. The poet shows the typical serious, courtly, and Christian (of a kind) attitude to these feasts. Gawain, out in the wilds on a perilous adventure, comes at last on Christmas Eve to a great castle, where he is courteously received by his host, taken to a warm room with a fire, offered a wash, and given splendid robes, since it was if anything more necessary to wear warm clothing inside a draughty medieval castle than outside it. Since Gawain has come after the main meal he eats on his own in his chamber. It is the eve of a feast and therefore a time of fast, so no meat but only fish can be served. The poet makes a nice blend of devotion and courtliness, in which of course there is no faintest trace of cynicism:

> Soon was raised up a table on trestles full fair,
> Clad with a clean cloth that clear white showed,
> Serviettes and salt-cellar and silvery spoons;
> The wight washed at his will, and went to his food.   *man*
> Servants him served seemly enough,
> With so many stews and suitable, seasoned of the best
> Double-fold, as it fell out, and many kinds of fishes
> Some baked in bread, some broiled on the coals,
> Some seethed, some in stew, savoured with spices,
> And always sauces so subtle that satisfied the knight.
> The knight called it a feast full freely and often,
> Very courteously, when all the gentlemen replied to him at once,
>   courteous too,
> 'This penance now you take
> Later shall amend.'
> The man much mirth did make,
> For wine to his head did wend.

> *Sir Gawain and the Green Knight*, ll. 884-900

(The modernisation, a necessary convenience even when the original is not very difficult, is a miserable travesty of the full effectiveness of the poetry.)

Sauces have been mentioned often as of the greatest importance. The reader may like to have one specimen among many. Cameline sauce was made of 'raisons of crowns' (which I do not understand), nuts, bread crusts, cloves, cinnamon, and of course ginger, powdered together and mixed with vinegar. The Franklin's 'sop in wine' was chiefly a sauce as already mentioned, and the 'chawdwyn' could also be adapted to a sauce.

The wines that accompanied these sumptuous feasts were of great variety. Of the New Year Feast in the beginning of *Sir Gawain* the poet says of the people present

> Each two had dishes twelve
> Good beer and bright wine both

which suggests that people had less delicate tastes than nowadays. Though everyone who could afford it drank wine there was no such elaboration or sophistication of manner connected with it as there is in England today, and as there was to some extent in the fourteenth century about such skills as butchering the dead game, on which the noblest prided themselves. The attitude to wine was very much that of the ordinary man in France today.

It will have been noticed that a special table had to be put up on trestles for Gawain's meal. This will suggest the scantiness of furniture in the houses of all classes compared with that in England today. Here again the comparison of medieval English life with modern times shows it in certain respects more like that of France and Italy, where houses are still relatively uncluttered with large upholstered furniture. Once again the houses of the peasants were bare indeed. Earthen floors, mud or plaster walls, all unadorned; a basket or two for clothes; a trestle table and stools; rough though not, to modern eyes, ugly pottery, with knives, and horn or wooden spoons; wooden or no plates (slices of bread, 'trenchers', being used); one or two flea-ridden wooden beds, with straw mattresses and blankets; this is the level at which the majority lived, though the very poor might have straw alone for bed and bedclothes. But of course above this could be found every gradation, from the meanest little luxury or convenience, a chest for clothes, a better blanket, a Sheffield knife, to the wild and wasteful magnificence of a prince. But at all levels there is a rather conspicuous lack of furniture. An esquire's will quoted by Miss Rickert[1] gives a list of the contents of his house in which he mentions a lot of bedding (always an important and expensive item), painted cloths, towels, washbasins, bronze pots and pans and the like, silver-gilt salt-cellars, three iron braziers for the fires, and boards and trestles for tables; he was moderately well-to-do, yet there is no mention of chairs, or even, as there frequently is, of beds. He must have had at least benches or stools, presumably so rough and cheap that they were disregarded. Even Troilus, when he goes to mope in his bedroom, seems to have nowhere to sit but on the bed, where his visitor Pandarus sits also. Yet Troilus's bedroom was fairly large, for when he went to it in despair at hearing that Criseyde was to go to the Greeks, he shut *every* door and window. Similarly when the lady is attempting to seduce Sir Gawain, and visits him in the morning when he is in bed, there is clearly nowhere else for her to sit but on the bed. This does not mean that there were no chairs anywhere, of course. John Russell, in *The Book of Nurture* already quoted from, gives elaborate instructions to the chamberlain, or valet, on how to look after his master, and there refers to cushions and a chair. Even in such a great house as is there implied, however, the private chamber is as much a bedroom as a sitting room. It has a bed and benches, and perhaps only one chair.

The furnishings of a couple of merchants' houses in London have been preserved in lists in wills, which are quoted by Miss Rickert. Beds and bedding are here as always important—everyone will remember the similar situation in Elizabethan and Jacobean England, and the famous second-best bed that Shakespeare left to his wife. What a pity it is that in all the great variety of records that survive about Chaucer's official life there is no copy of his will. It would at least have given us an interesting glimpse of his status and circum-

[1] Edith Rickert, *Chaucer's World*, ed. C. C. Olson and M. M. Crow, Oxford University Press, 1948, p. 59.

stances at the time of his death. Thomas Mocking, a merchant whose will Miss Rickert quotes, had an eight-roomed house. In the bedroom were two beds, quite a lot of bedding, including feather-beds and pillows and sheets, and a couple of chests for clothes; no chairs. In the hall, which was the common living and eating room, there were the two trestles and the board for the table, five stools, and a lot of cushions. Perhaps the cushions were used for sitting on the floor. In a poem by Machaut, describing as an allegory a great man at home in France in the middle part of the century, the lord and several ladies all seem to be sitting around on the floor being read to. It is possible that this is how Criseyde and her ladies are to be imagined when Pandarus finds them within the 'paved parlour' at Criseyde's house, having read to them the Tale of Thebes. In Thomas Mocking's hall there were no less than seven washbowls, which would be used for the family and visitors to wash their hands in before they sat down to eat. It is a provision worth remembering when our ancestors are condemned as sweaty and unwashed, though whether anybody but the eccentric washed at all frequently beyond face and hands is another question. The pantry had a cupboard, and contained plates, jugs, spoons, etc., of pewter and a few of silver. The parlour had no seats, but a dorser or dosser, which was a piece of cloth to hang over the back of a chair or against a wall; and a banker, which is a bench-cover. It also had quite literally a cup-board—a board, presumably a shelf, on which cups were kept. The workmen's room had merely a chest and a board; the apprentices' room had a board, perhaps for use as a table, and four benches. Only in the room next to the parlour were there three chairs, perhaps to be taken out when visitors came. The kitchen had a board for a bench and a fine array of pots, pans, spits, tripods, gridirons, a frying pan, a sieve, and so forth for cooking. In this will the total value of the furnishings is £238 16s. 3d., which is a vast sum by modern standards.

The furnishings of a great house would be much the same as these, only on a larger scale, while the Royal household was vast indeed. Even there the tables had normally to be put up and taken down for each meal. (Chaucer's Franklin is exceptional for he has 'standing tables' on which food remains all day. Such a table was a luxury that was beginning to become common in Flanders.) A contemporary says that Richard's household steward fed ten thousand people a day, and while this is obviously an exaggeration, the constant Parliamentary complaints of the size and extravagance of the royal household under Richard certainly bears out the general impression it gives. A great house was distinguished by the number and beauty of the silver and gold cups, salt-cellars and bowls which it had, and these items are constantly recorded among possessions and as gifts to courtiers like Chaucer and his wife. Such worked and enamelled objects, practically all of them now perished, were, to judge from the few survivors, of very great beauty. Another

Kitchen scene – pounding meat, stirring paste

item found in notable splendour in great households was the hangings to go on the walls. These may have had some effect against draughts, but were chiefly for decoration. On them were embroidered or woven all sorts of stories from Romance, and decorative scenes in general. (In less rich houses such scenes were painted on the walls as frescoes.) Beds and bedding, too, were correspondingly rich. The slightly humorous list of splendid bedding that Chaucer vows to Morpheus in *The Book of the Duchess* is not so unrealistic (or perhaps so funny) as might be assumed. An example of all these things may be found in the Black Prince's will, written in French, of which I translate a few representative extracts, by no means complete. It is a document of great interest to the social historian, which seems to have had little attention paid to it.

The Black Prince first gives very detailed instructions for his tomb and for the splendid sombre procession in which his body is to be taken to Canterbury; then he comes to the bequests to various

ooking stews (note double saucepans), roasting birds

churches and chapels; for example to the chapel of Our Lady where he is to lie he bequeathes his white garment diapered all over with the pattern of a vine in blue, and also the altar-frontal which the Bishop of Exeter gave him, which has the Assumption of Our Lady in the middle enclosed in gold, and other pictures. Then he comes to some tapestry; a whole length of tapestry, enough to go right round a room, was called a Hall:

Item, we give and assign our Hall of ostrich plumes and black tapestry [he had a fondness for black, which was the colour of his armour at Crécy—hence the nickname that the French and later the English gave him] and with a red border, with swans with the heads of ladies; that is to say, a dosser, and eight pieces for the sides, and two bankers, to the said church of Canterbury. . . .

Item, we give and assign the remainder of all our clothing, cloth of gold, the tabernacle of the Resurrection, two shrines of silver-gilt enamelled in the same way, crosses, chalices, vessels for the wine and water of the Eucharist, candelabras, basins, liveries [i.e. suits of clothes worn by his servants], and all our other ornaments belonging to Holy Church to our chapel of St Nicholas within our castle of Wallingford, to be used and remain there perpetually . . . always excepted the blue garment with the roses of gold and the ostrich plumes, the which garment, complete, with all that belongs to it we give and assign to our son Richard, together with the bed which we have of the same pattern, and all the apparel of the said bed, which our honoured lord and father the King gave us.

Item, we give and assign to our said son our bed striped with baudekyn [a rich, embroidered cloth, half of the threads being in gold] and red camaca [a fine cloth like silk] which is quite new, with all that belongs to the said bed.

Item, we give and assign to our said son our great bed with the embroidered angels, with the cushions, blankets, coverlet, sheets, and all the other apparel belonging to the said bed.

Item, we give and assign to our said son the Hall of arras, with the pass of Saladin [? some story about the great Saracen enemy of the Crusaders]; and also the Hall of worsted, embroidered with mermaids of the sea and with the edge of red striped with black, and embroidered with swans with the heads of women, and with ostrich feathers; the which Halls we desire that our said son should have with all that belongs to them. . . .

Item, we give and assign to our said consort the Princess the red Hall of worsted, embroidered with eagles and griffins, with the edging of swans with the heads of women.

Item, we assign to Sir Roger de Clarendon [his illegitimate son] a bed of silk at the discretion of our executors, with all that belongs to the said bed.

Item, we give and assign to Sir Robert de Walsham, our confessor, a great bed of red camaca with our arms embroidered at each corner (and the said camaca is diapered in the same way with the arms of Hereford), together with the whole canopy, curtains, cushions, coverlet, coverings of tapestry, and the whole of the rest of the apparel.

There is yet another bed for one of his executors, of white camaca embroidered with azure eagles, but enough is here to suggest the type of court luxury, and the kinds of ways in which, as regards furniture, it revealed itself. It is the furniture of people active, not accustomed to hang round the house all day, or to be much concerned with sedentary pursuits. When, as with Troilus, they were princes of the blood who sought such privacy as they could get within their bedrooms, they flung themselves down on splendid and colourful works of art, and gazed upon storied walls, richly dight.

Such surroundings must have been a help in times of sickness, for when people were ill they had to stay at home. Hospitals were not places of medical science but refuges for the destitute and the helpless, where sick people might indeed be looked after, but with no greater skill than at home. Most people were born, were ill, and died, in their own beds at home, with little privacy or solitude. This was probably quite good for their emotional welfare. Anyone who has known, especially as a child, the miserable depersonalisation imposed on patients in a modern English hospital, will realise the

Doctors with patient   Nurse and patient

benefits of being treated as a human being when ill, and of being kept in a human group. But it may not be very hygienic. In the case of infectious diseases, and diseases like the Plague, which are carried by fleas, the lack of isolation was disastrous to health.

If a person was ill, the normal treatment no doubt was for a member of the family, or some reputable person in the neighbourhood, to prescribe a traditional medicine. Then as now there was a natural amateur concern with such matters. Most educated men had some interest in medicine, and might easily inherit, or compile, a list of remedies. Chaucer's interest was as usual thoroughly intellectual. He seems to have mastered the principles as they were then known, probably from the encyclopaedia of Vincent of Beauvais. He made use of his knowledge in the descriptions of Arcite's wound in *The Knight's Tale*. He was also aware of the common social judgements of doctors, of their greed for money, their collusion with the apothecaries who made up prescriptions. Henry of Lancaster is another example of educated interest in medicine, with his *Livre de Seyntz Medicines*, though he uses medical matters as a metaphor for moral matters. A rather more typical and more purely medical compilation is found in the Thornton Manuscript, described more fully later

(p. 130), which has a list of remedies. They are traditional, copied and recopied from manuscripts, going back to the original Greek masters, but muddled rather than improved by the passage of time. They usually consist of relatively common herbs ground up and boiled, then taken internally or externally; though there are other ingredients more startling, that are often used as well. For sore eyes, for example, boiled slug-juice is recommended. The sixteen different remedies for toothache include laying to the tooth rubbed straw-berry stalks, pepper, or the filth of a badger—the latter, we are assured, will break the tooth and so stop the pain. Another remedy for 'worms in the teeth' reads:

> Take the seeds of henbane and the seeds of leeks and frankincense, and lay all these on a glowing tile-stone; and make a pipe that has a wide and a narrow end, and set the narrow end to thy tooth, and lay the seeds and frankincense upon the hot tile-stone, and set the wide end of the pipe upon them; and let the vapour from them strike up through the pipe on to thy tooth, and it shall slay the worms and stop the pain.[1]

The remedy for another unpleasant ailment requires the powder of a burnt felt hat. One of the ways to stop nose-bleeding is to burn eel-skins and to blow the powder up the sufferer's nose with a pipe. These remedies may make us grateful for the advances of medical science, but not all these ancient medicines were quite absurd. Hen-bane, for example, is a plant with narcotic properties, and so may have been some help in deadening pain. That these remedies, or others like them, occasionally persist even today among elderly peo-ple in remote districts does not mean that they originate with 'the folk'—it is a romantic fallacy to suppose that many things do. They are a learned tradition, and Thornton gives as his authority for several of his prescriptions the Rector of Oswaldkirk, who was his local parson, and obviously a learned man. Another prescription is attri-

---

[1] Modernised from *Liber de Diversis Medicinibus*, ed. by Margaret S. Ogden, Early English Text Society, O.S. 207, Oxford University Press, 1938.

buted to 'Ser Apilton'. This is thought to be William Appleton, a friar, who was a doctor employed by John of Gaunt. His prescription is much more elaborate and expensive than most of the others, though essentially of the same kind. The rich could afford rare and strange ingredients, Eastern spices and ointments, costing huge sums. Some medicines for the rich had more than fifty ingredients.

It was only the rich who could afford doctors. Chaucer's description in the *General Prologue* of his Doctor of Physic hints pretty broadly how expensive doctors were. It is often thought that Chaucer's description may be based on his knowledge of the most famous doctor of his day, John Arderne, who wrote a treatise *De Fistula*[1] which gives a lot of information not only on strictly surgical matters but on how a doctor should behave, and what fees he should get. Arderne says that a doctor should never ask too little—it is bad for the patient as well as for the practitioner. He should also get his fee before he begins the cure—a wise precaution in those days. For the operation in which he specialises Arderne says he asks an important man forty pounds, plus robes and fees amounting to five pounds a year for life. In any case a doctor should never take less than five pounds, which was more than most people earned in a year. All these sums should be multiplied by sixty for a rough equivalent to today's values. Besides advising how to develop a good bedside manner and maintain a good reputation, Arderne emphasises also the astrological basis of scientific medicine, just as Chaucer does in his portrait of the Doctor. Although astrology seems pure nonsense to us, it was the basis of much of the most advanced science in the fourteenth century, and Chaucer's Doctor is not a quack for believing it.

Chaucer's satire of the Doctor is that of a literary man, and echoes the general literary opinion of the century, from courtly writers like

[1] Edited by D'Arcy Power, Early English Text Society, O.S. 139, Oxford University Press, 1910.

Chaucer and Gower to the preachers and Langland. This sort of distrust of experts who make a good thing out of their expertise is natural in every century, and there is no reason to believe that, science apart, doctors were any worse in the fourteenth century than they are now. The rich always get better medical treatment than the poor; that is one of the many facts that give meaning to the distinction between rich and poor. The rich man had the further advantage of a bedroom, a bed, warmth, a good roof, and plenty of servants. The poor man had none of this to help him bear the burden of sickness.

Even a rich man's house was not all sweetness and light, and one final darker touch must be added to complete this series of sketches of home-life and related matters. No contemporary makes this point, to my knowledge, but Erasmus, over a century later, commented on the filthiness of the streets in England, and especially of the floors of houses. True, he made the same complaints about Paris. The floors, he says, are usually of clay, upon which are placed rushes, which are occasionally added to but never changed. They remain for twenty years, warming beneath them spittle, vomit, urine, spilt beer, the remains of fish, and other filth not to be mentioned. This would be in the hall, where people ate, rather than in the other rooms, but still it gives point to the foot-cloth that John Russell's valet must put down on the ground for his master to step on to when he dressed, even in his own chamber; hence the point of Chaucer mentioning that Criseyde's parlour was paved—it showed how fine it was. When a knight was being armed, of which there is colourful description in *Sir Gawain*, it was customary to put down a rich cloth on which he stood and on which the armour was laid. When the armour had been 'rocked', that is, rolled, to free the rust, and polished and oiled, one would not want it to pick up the mess on the floor, yet there were few or no standing tables on which one could put down things of bulk until they were needed. Yet the occasional evidence for sitting on the floor suggests that not all floors were so nasty, and it is possible that the fourteenth century was not so bad in this respect as the sixteenth, though I must confess that it seems rather more likely that the fourteenth century simply had not produced a man so sensitive as Erasmus. We may remember how Swift brought, as we may say, a modern nose to the smells of eighteenth-century London, to his own great discomfort. It is rarely convenient to be in advance of the hygiene of one's times. There can be little doubt that fourteenth-century London stank, and so did fourteenth-century Londoners, but it did not worry them, and luckily need not worry us.

All the same, there is no need to exaggerate. It has been noted that people, at any rate of the upper classes, washed frequently if not copiously, though in many cases they washed without soap. All courts and magnates' households seem to have had a plentiful supply of washerwomen, while at the other end of the scale it is clear that women in the country hung out their washing to dry on the hedge and had it stolen long before Falstaff's men came along; in the early fourteenth-century comic poem, *The Man in the Moon*, the thief is the man in the moon himself. Soap must have been precious, and for the most part made at home from fat and wood-ash, though it could also be bought. Dirtiness must be measured, as a moral quality, by the difficulty of keeping clean, as well as by the prevailing opinion (Dr Johnson once confessed to having no love for clean linen). Most people, again, must have suffered from fleas, and it is always said that the inns were full of them, but no one would choose to suffer from such an affliction if the means of avoiding it were at hand. There were no disinfectants of any kind. And if you sleep in straw it is impossible to remain free from bugs.

The poor were dirty. In the early fifteenth-century romance, *Syr Generides*, a princess is escaping in the disguise of a washerwoman, wearing clothes tucked up higher than her normal ground-length dresses. Her helper tells her that her white legs will betray them, and so rubs her legs with ashes to bring them to the dinginess of the normal washerwoman. It would be a matter, to some extent, of exposure. A peasant woman, out in all weathers, clad in short clothes suitable for heavy work, was deeply tanned as well as dirty. The lady, who went out little, was covered up in long heavy clothes. She cherished the extreme whiteness of her skin, as all ladies did until as recently as thirty or forty years ago. It is a modern wish to have one's skin look like brown leather. In the light of this sort of thing it is easier to relish the vivid though controlled realism in *The Clerk's Tale*, where Chaucer tells how the Marquis has chosen Griselda, the poorest girl in the village, for his wife, and orders the court ladies to look after her:

> Of which thise ladyes were nat right glad
> To handle hir clothes, wherinne she was clad.
> But nathelees, this mayde bright of hewe   *none the less*
> Fro foot to heed they clothed han al newe.   *have*
> Hir heris han they kembd, that lay untressed   *hair; combed; unplaited*
> Full rudely.   *roughly*
>
>   *The Clerk's Tale*, CT IV, ll. 375-80

But again the most vivid picture of the poor man's lot comes from a religious and alliterative writer of the time, inspired by Lollardy and Langland; he is the unknown author of *Pierce the Ploughman's Crede*, written between 1393 and 1400. He has a remarkable passage which I quote here (as usual a little modernised) because it is an unusually detailed account of dress; but the vigour, humanity, and indignation of the passage are also interesting.

> As I went by the way weeping for sorrow
> I saw a simple man by me upon the plough hanging,
> His coat was of a rough cloth that cary was called,
> His hood was full of holes and his hair was out,
> With his worn shoes cobbled full thick;

His toes stuck out as he the land trod,
His hose overhung his hocks on every side,
All bemired in mud as he the plough followed;
Two mittens, as meanly made all of rough cloth;
The fingers were worn out, and full of clinging filth.
This wight wallowed in the mud almost to the ankle;
Four heifers in front of him that feeble were become;
Men might reckon each rib, so wretched they were.
His wife walked by him, with a long goad,
In a cut coat, caught up full high,
Wrapped in a winnowing-sheet to ward off the weather,
Barefoot on the bare ice so that blood followed.
And at the land's end lay a little crumb-bowl,
And there-in lay a little child, lapped in rags,
And two of two years old upon another side,
And all they sang one song that sorrow was to hear;
They cried all one cry, a care-full note.
The simple man sighed sore and said, 'Children, be quiet!'

Langland himself has one or two pictures of poor men in their rags which bring home once again the state, not of the destitute, but of the ordinary poor; but there is hardly space to quote them. Grey or russet were the universal colours of the peasants' clothing. Women wore a shift and over that usually, but not always, a rough outer garment. Men wore a sort of loincloth, or primitive drawers, called a 'breche', and over that a tunic, and/or the rough sleeveless smock called a tabard, which in more ornamented form was also the dress of the herald.

The variety and colour increases so greatly as we move up the social scale that it is hardly possible to do more than hint at it. Before making the attempt three general points should be made. The first is that there were far greater differences in the dress of different classes of men and women then than there are nowadays. In the fourteenth century there was even legislation to try to preserve the difference in dress between the social ranks, of which at least seven grades were distinguished. The different trades had different manners of dress. The clergy differed from the rest of the people and among themselves in fashion of garment, wearing black, white, brown and grey colours. The elderly tended to dress markedly differently from the young—compare the portrait of the elderly Chaucer (p. 198) with that of the young squire (p. 110). When we come to the court, it is clear that courtiers vied with each other in the richness and fancifulness of their dress (though it is not true that the toes of shoes were worn so long that they had to be hooked back to the shin with a little gold chain!).

The second point is that throughout the century, for all the wishes of legislators, there was a general development of fashion, though this did not affect the peasants. There are two chief trends; one is the almost inevitable human trend, at any rate in England, for lower classes to copy the dress of the higher classes; it is an aspect of that

The dress of a middle-aged lady

Left The angel Gabriel as an elegant young man of the fourteenth century.
Painted oak
Right The Virgin Mary as an elegant young woman of the fourteenth century.
Painted oak

social climbing and petty snobbery which is one of the most valuable
of the social stabilisers that help to preserve society. Moralists, however, of all kinds, have always disapproved of the lower classes aping
their betters. There is an early fourteenth-century lyric in the famous
Harley Manuscript 2253, entitled by editors *The Follies of Fashion*,
which complains about 'gigelots' aping ladies of high fashion.
Chroniclers make similar complaints. The other general trend is in
the design of clothes themselves, which as the century progressed
began to cling more closely to the figure, and to reveal more of its
shape, with both men and women. This tendency was helped by
the development of finer fabrics, though never did the Middle Ages
develop the very softly-flowing flexible materials that some historical
films would have us believe. For all this tendency towards 'natural-
ism', however, there was still plenty of fanciful costume, with long
pointed shoes for young men, and pointed, trailing sleeves, that easily
went into the dirt. And in general clothing was not very practical.
Even armour was cluttered up with flowing robes. It was these
robes catching in his spurs that caused the death of Sir John Chandos,
as Froissart describes in one of his vivid passages. In 'civilian' clothes,
even elderly men must surely have found the long robe such as
Chaucer wears in the Harley portrait a great inconvenience, though
warmer to the leg than fashionable hose, or the red and black breeches
and short cloak which the Countess Elizabeth bought for Chaucer
when he was her page in 1357.

The third point concerns style. Every period has a general style
which is reflected as much in clothes as in literature, painting, or
architecture. It has long been recognised that there is a surprisingly
close connection between the style of clothes and that of architecture.
In the latter part of the fourteenth century the architectural style
was Gothic, within which 'Perpendicular' was developing out of
'Decorated'. Frequently the functional structure of churches and
poems and clothes was overlaid with swarming lively detail, in-

Left The Lady of the Castle visits Sir Gawain in bed. Her hair is held in a jewelled net of very open design, called a Tressour. Compare its pattern with the lierne vaulting of Gloucester Cathedral Choir   *Right* Lierne vaulting, second quarter of the fourteenth century, Gloucester Cathedral Choir

creasingly realistic and varied, often grotesque and humorous. Such detail gives a constantly interesting texture, but obscures function and main structure. So it is sometimes with Chaucer's and Langland's poetry, and so it was with clothes. It is difficult for us, in a period of perhaps the most utilitarian style that our history has known, to respond easily to such quantities of fanciful, and as it may seem, irresponsible and irrelevant decoration. We can hardly restrain our impatience at the rich clothes of either sex slopped in the dirt, failing even to keep their wearers warm, tripping them up, and costing huge sums. (In this we agree with the condemnation of the preachers and moralists.) Yet the Gothic style as a whole has its noble aspirations as well as its grotesqueries and impracticalities. Its sharp angles and springing lines, its complex patterns and unashamed enjoyment of colour, found their noblest expression in the Gothic

The Nave, Canterbury Cathedral, looking East

Left The Percy Tomb at Beverley Minster shows the decorative inventiveness of Gothic architecture of the 'fifties and 'sixties *Right* A fashionable young man, late fourteenth century. The lion and the sun (?) are superimposed astrological images

cathedrals. If we judge the style of an age by its most characteristic products, we must compare the cathedral or even the parish church of the Gothic period with the office-blocks and dead city-centres of the present day. We must compare the robes of red silk, bordered with white and embroidered with gold, with Savile Row lounge suits and plus-fours. In minor aspects of style we must compare the joyous or sometimes morbid inventiveness of Gothic detail with the blank slabs and repetitious modules of modern architecture. I am not suggesting that the present age can or should do other than it does. Nothing is more tiresome than broad condemnations of the present in comparison with the past. But the past rewards the sympathetic interest of the present with suggestions of otherwise unknown modes of being. So we may appreciate what we do not want, or at any rate cannot have. In clothing of the fourteenth century we may recognise that the gaiety and splendour are part of a lovely style, and that while they no doubt ministered to vanity they were not *merely* vain; they were a genuine contribution to the gaiety and splendour of life itself. And men contributed as much as women. The virtue of the well-dressed man was not, as it has been since Beau Brummell, that his clothes were not noticed. Very much the reverse. Men were peacocks, and the colourful clothes of the well-to-do expressed their station in life, their occupation, personal character, and self-confidence.

The illustrations will show quicker and better than my words the variety of dress that people might wear; and in words the descriptions of variety of dress have been done superbly, once and for all, in the *General Prologue* to *The Canterbury Tales*. To conclude this chapter I shall pick out a few items about clothing and make-up that the pictures do not show. The will of the London grocer, Richard Toky, quoted by Miss Rickert in her invaluable compilation, has a long list of clothing, which contains a few items of special interest. One is a nightshirt, a rare item when most people slept naked. Another, not rare, is a nightcap. A more general point is the greater proportion of outer to underclothing. Such underclothes as there were were slight, and perhaps not changed as often as a more fastidious age might wish; also, heavy clothes had to be worn in the house as I have already suggested. John Russell's valet is told to make sure his master finds ready for him when he gets up a clean shirt and hose, socks, a tunic, a doublet, and a long coat if he wants it. The hose were stockings joined at the top and going up to the waist, like men's long pants today. The lord might also wear a 'pauncher', which presumably was a broad band of warm material such as men often wear round their middles in the colder parts of the East today. On top of all this he may wear a robe or gown, and a cloak or cape 'for the house'. Outside he would add a hood or hat. While he is being dressed, the master stands on a footsheet, and when he is dressed a kerchief is placed on his shoulders and his hair is combed;

finally he is offered warm water with which to wash his hands and face. When he undresses for bed there is no mention of washing nor of nightshirt, though there is of a kerchief and nightcap. A chamber-pot and night-stool are set. Finally, the curtains are drawn around the bed, and a nightlight (which would be in a basin of water) is set to last the whole night. Then the valet drives out the dog and the cat 'giving them a clout', and bows good night to his lord.

We have occasionally come across references to washing, and it is clear that the usual custom among the upper classes was to wash in plain water on getting up, and before meals. Occasionally they bathed, though bathing was usually associated with not being well. John Russell gives some interesting directions for when the lord wishes to take a bath. Sheets are to be hung about the roof, full of flowers and sweet green herbs. Then the lord, undressed, sits on a large sponge covered by a sheet (the door being carefully shut) and places his feet upon another large sponge. Other sponges are set

A gentleman dressing by the fire

about for him to rest on. Then the valet takes a basinful of hot herbs (presumably in water, though that is not mentioned) and with a soft sponge washes the lord. Then he must throw warm rose-water over his lord, who may then go to the fire where he stands on his foot-sheet to be dried with a clean cloth. Then take him to bed, says Russell, to cure his troubles. One can see that such an elaborate business might not be undertaken too often. No private house had a bathroom, of course, and though Paris, Florence, and other Continental cities had bath-houses, I can find no reference to a public bath-house in England at this time.

It will also be noticed that Russell, who elsewhere is so detailed as to give instructions for keeping the privy clean (cloth, not lavatory paper, was used) makes no mention of shaving. Practically all men in the fourteenth and fifteenth centuries wore beards. When Arcita makes his vows to Mars in *The Knight's Tale*, he says that his beard and hair have never felt the 'offence' of razor or of shears, and that they hang down long, as we may well believe.[1] Chaucer, as we know from the portrait procured by Hoccleve, wore a beard. But monks certainly had their tonsures made by shaving, and in the Household Ordinances of Edward IV, which date from later in the fifteenth century but are usually thought to reflect earlier times, it is said that the King may wish to be shaved on Saturday nights. In Chaucer's poetry to be clean-shaven is a sign of effeminacy with the Pardoner, who has no beard; and of eccentricity or of a particular kind of shabby-smartness with the Reeve. To be clean-shaven is also a sign of absurd or wrongful amorousness; the lecherous monk in *The Shipman's Tale* turns up all smart 'with crown [i.e. tonsure] and beard newly shaven', while the old knight in *The Merchant's Tale* 'was shaven all new in his manner'—so that the thick hard bristles

[1] It is an interesting fact for social history that the word 'scissors' is first recorded in Chaucer, in connection with trimming beards (HF 690). The things had been known as shears from Old English times; they were acquiring a new fancy French name.

were like the skin of a dog-fish, sharp as briars. Obviously Chaucer felt a beard to be the manly, decent thing. But men, as well as women, at least at court, also had their hair curled, and it is to be doubted if the Squire's curly locks were natural.

Chaucer also had views, it would appear, on the use of make-up. In the French poem, *Le Roman de la Rose*, part of which Chaucer probably translated when he was a young man, there is near the beginning the description of a lady called Beauty, and Chaucer adds to his translation the lines

> No wyndred browis hadde she,   *plucked eyebrows*
> Ne popped hir, for it neded nought   *painted herself*
> To wyndre hir, or to peynte hir ought.

Like many men he seems to have disapproved of female make-up, though there is no reason to suppose that such a view was much regarded then or at any other time by those whom it most concerned.

What is more surprising to us is that it seems to have been fairly common for men at court to use make-up, and that Chaucer does not seem to disapprove of this. When the bird-heroine of *The Squire's Tale* describes the courtly bird who so loved her, as she thought, she says,

> His manere was an hevene for to see
> Til any woman, were she never so wys,   *for*
> So peynted he and kembde at point-devys   *combed to perfection*
> As wel his wordes as his contenaunce.

The Squire's Tale, CT V, ll. 558-61

And the cheerful Host, when he is praising the burly, high-coloured Nun's Priest after the story of Chanticleer, says of him,

> Him nedeth nat his colour for to dyen   *dye*
> With brasile, ne with greyn of Portyngale.

CT VII, ll. 3458-9

Brasil and greyn are red dyes which were imported from Portugal.

As the ideal of beauty for both men and women included yellow hair, white skin, and rosy-red cheeks (Canacee's beauty is compared with the red rising sun) it is clear that both sexes were inclined to aid nature with a little strong red dye. Other adornments were usual. Henry of Lancaster in *Le Livre de Seyntz Medicines* says how proud he was not only of the strength and beauty of his hands, but of the beautiful rings he wore; how proud he was of beautiful stirrups, shoes and garters; and adds how he loved the sweet smell of ladies' scent, and also, rather oddly, how he loved the smell of scarlet cloth.

Lastly, a brief word must be said about the clothing of such clerics as have already been mentioned in passing. By the end of the fourteenth century the rule for many monks, who were supposed to be enclosed away from the world, was much relaxed, and some of them, as we have seen, might have been met on the highways or in the houses of rich friends. Friars had never been enclosed; it was their job to live in the world. And the so-called secular clergy were those priests, and clerics of rank lower than priests, whose duty it was to look after the souls of men in the world and to live amongst them. The clothes of all these orders were the familiar long gowns with hoods, of different cuts and colours, but fundamentally alike. The manners of the secular clergy and friars were much the same as those of lay people as to washing and so forth, except that they were supposed to have the crowns of their heads shaved, originally as a disfigurement to mortify the flesh and avoid the vanity of the world. Sometimes clerics deliberately neglected the tonsure so that it became hardly noticeable, but it is clear from the monk in *The Shipman's Tale* that sometimes a natty, freshly-shaved tonsure was regarded as a mark of smartness. Some monastic orders limited the amount of washing that their members might undertake simply to mortify the flesh, not from any liking for dirt. But the Austin Canons who were a semi-regular body, and the most numerous in England, were distinguished by their insistence on cleanliness, and also by being allowed to wear linen next to their skins, as only the upper class could afford to do. The lower classes because they had no choice, and monks to mortify the flesh, wore, or were supposed to wear, wool next to their skins. The extremely ascetic, such as recluses, and even specially pious lay-folk, sometimes wore hair-shirts under their clothes, or even under armour. These could be so rough as to draw blood, as is told of Sir Thomas More in the early sixteenth century.

We are left with an impression of extreme variety in this brief and inevitably sketchy survey of the domestic side of medieval life. In some respects this variety was not so great as it seems, because most people were peasants, free or unfree, and the possibilities open to them were limited. But once one considers the levels of society above the great labouring mass, then, especially as far as dress is concerned, there is no doubt that for good and bad the variation between old and young, rich and poor, secular and religious, was much greater, and often more revealing of occupation and character, than in the present age.

CHAPTER FIVE

Growing Up

WHEN a child was born, it was wrapped up like a little
mummy, as can be seen from manuscript illuminations.
Since so many children died it is understandable that people were
intensely conscious of the frailty of the very young, but unfortunately in a pre-scientific age they took the wrong means to guard
them. So a baby was wrapped up tight in the belief that if he waved
his frail limbs about he might break them. In this respect the children of the poor who were not so swathed had a more favourable
chance than those better off, and it is perhaps from practices like
these that there arises the idea that poorer people are stronger and
coarser than their 'betters'.

The babies of the better off, then as for several centuries to come,
were usually put out to a wet-nurse. It cannot have been very
difficult to find a woman whose own suckling had just died, and
sometimes a poor woman might suckle her own child and a stran-
ger's. It was thought that the quality of milk a child received might
affect its character, but in fact no one seems to have bothered much
about such matters. Nevertheless, common sentiments were, as one
would expect, tender to babies, and Chaucer agrees well with the
spirit of his times when he draws a touching picture of Constance
with her little child, and gives her such tender, even sentimental,
speeches.

Yet what Chaucer and his contemporaries found so affecting was
the total group of mother-and-child. It was an age when the ideal
of the social or family group was still stronger than that of the
isolated individual—as it was for several centuries to come.

Baby wrapped up in the cradle

A child was probably suckled for a long time, like the children of the Egyptians in Moses' time, and those of Japanese peasants to-day, who are suckled till four or five. Once past the baby stage the child was in effect treated as if he were an ignorant grown-up, and attempts were made to discipline him accordingly. He was continually admonished into a preternaturally sober and controlled way of life. Of course, the common nature of childhood was recognised, its wildness, its incapacity for prolonged attention, and so forth, but these were considered to be sinful failings, and punished with the stick or whip. On the other hand, some things eased this harshness. Adults in medieval society were themselves less inhibited, more childish, and more inconsistent than educated modern English people. Their rules must have had many lapses, and impulsive violence to-wards children, of which there was so much, was no doubt often made up for by equally impulsive demonstrations of love. The general medieval inefficiency, the astonishingly wide gulf that so often existed between rule and practice, must always be remembered when, as so often, evidence of the rules is so much easier to come by than evidence of what actually happened, except when that was irregular enough to be brought before the law-courts or to be commented upon by writers. Our own society, if looked at entirely through cases reaching the magistrates and judges, would hardly show up well. One must remember the great mass of ordinary sensible people who achieved some sort of way of life following their own temperaments and compromising as best they might with their principles and the wilfulness of their children.

There was practically no idea of personal development. A child, it seems to have been thought, could be responsible, if he would. And if he wouldn't, he ought to be beaten. It is significant that there was no word corresponding to our word 'naughty'. The word 'naught(y)' itself already existed, but, as still in Shakespeare's time, it meant 'wicked'. So, as the good wife taught her daughter,

> And if thy children be rebel, and will not them bow,
> If any of them misdo, neither curse them nor blow,
> But take a smart rod and beat them on a row
> Till they cry mercy, and be of their guilt aknow.
>
> *acknowledge their guilt*

All this may be illustrated from Bartholomew the Englishman, in Trevisa's translation; first he deals with the little child, that is, one up to seven years old; then he treats of the child between seven and fourteen, from the time 'when he is weaned from milk and knoweth good and evil'

and therefore he is able to receive punishment and learning, and then he is put and set to learning under tutors, and compelled to take learning and punishment. . . . (Such children are pure, and know nothing of sex.) . . . Then such children are soft of flesh, lithe and pliant of body, quick and light to move, intelligent enough to learn, and they lead their lives without thought and care, and set their hearts only on mirth and pleasure, and dread no perils more than beating with a rod, and they love an apple more than gold . . . they are quickly and soon angry, and soon pleased, and easily they forgive; and because of tenderness of body

119

they are soon hurt and grieved, and cannot well endure hard work . . .
they move lightly, and are unsteadfast and unstable. Through great
and strong heat they desire much food, and so by reason of excess of
food and drink they fall often and many times into various sicknesses
and evils. And those children which be gendered and begotten of corrupt father and mother take corruption from them . . . when children's
voice changeth it is a token of puberty, and then they are able to gender
and beget children.

Since all children are spotted with evil manners, and think on things
that be, and regard not of things that shall be, they love playing, and
games, and vanity, and forsake learning and profit; and things most
worthy they repute least worthy, and least worthy most worthy. They
desire things that be to them contrary and grievous, and set more store
by the image of a child than the image of a man, and make more sorrow
and woe, and weep more for the loss of an apple, than for the loss of their
heritage; and the goodness that is done for them they let it pass out of
mind. They desire all things that they see, and pray and ask with voice
and with hand. They love talking and counsel of such children as they
be, and avoid company of old men. They keep no counsel, but they
tell all they hear or see. Suddenly they laugh and suddenly they weep.
Always they cry, jangle, scorn, or disdain, that hardly they be still while
they sleep. When they are washed of filth, straightaway they defile
themselves again. When the mother washeth and combeth them, they
kick and sprawl, and put with feet and with hands, and withstandeth
with all their might. For they think only on belly joy.

This certainly speaks to a modern parent's heart; but what we think
of as a child's nature, to which we must, to some extent, adapt its
education and circumstances, they thought of as a child's nature
which must be sharply corrected to suit the circumstances. The
frequency with which crying is referred to when discussing children
is surely greater in the fourteenth century than it would be today.
No one in the fourteenth century ever thinks, even in extreme
sentimentality, of childhood as being 'the happiest time of one's
life'. Yet again, we must not paint too black a picture. Froissart

describes his own childhood and the fifty-odd games he played (many of them known today) very cheerfully, while we have a not unpleasant picture of a late fourteenth-century childhood described in an autobiographical passage by the monk and poet, John Lydgate, who was born about 1370.

Lydgate says the time of his childhood extended to his fifteenth year, and it was a time of many 'unbridled passions'. He gives an account much like Bartholomew's of his wildness, his passionateness, dislike of virtue, reluctance to learn, fear only of the rod, impudence, obstinacy, and so on. He stole apples and grapes and played cherry-stones rather than go to church. He was loath to get up in the morning, and even more reluctant to go to bed at night, hated prayers, was rude to those who corrected him, and wouldn't wash his hands before dinner. He hated school. He tells all this with something of the smugness of a virtuous man who likes to show that he too is human, and who, moreover, has mended his ways. It suggests that for all the repressiveness of the system there were then as now plenty of ways for a high-spirited boy to get round it.

Just how high-spirited boys were is shown by their games. A twelfth-century writer, Fitzstephen, wrote a famous description of London, which Stow quotes as still holding good in many parts as late as the sixteenth century. Fitzstephen has a famous passage on the games of Londoners, when all classes used to go out into the fields close by on holidays and Sundays, and on Fridays when there was usually a great horse fair. The older people watched and often urged on the games of the younger ones. Girls took part as well as boys, though their games were less violent, and all they are recorded as doing is dancing until moonrise. The smaller children played with balls (as did the city officials) and the bigger ones in summer played at archery practice, running, jumping, wrestling, putting the stone, slings, duelling with shields and swords. They also played with split spear-shafts (lighter than the unsplit shaft) from which the

Boys' games – mock battles

iron war-heads had been removed, imitating the war-like practices of their elders. In winter-time, when the swamp outside the north wall of the city was frozen over, crowds of boys went on to the ice. Sometimes they just played at sliding; at other times they made a sled of a lump of ice, and a whole crowd of boys would make a chain and pull the one on the sled. Sometimes the whole lot slipped and fell in a heap. Others fixed the thigh bones of animals to their feet, to make primitive skates, and pushed themselves along with sticks tipped with iron. They could get up a great speed in this way, and sometimes two boys would dash at each other from far apart, and crash into each other, skinning and bruising themselves, sometimes even breaking an arm or a leg, which was a serious matter in days before scientific medicine. 'But,' says Fitzstephen, 'youth is eager for glory, youth is greedy for victory, and in order to be the braver in real battles, they practise these mock battles.' Mock battles, though not on ice, were particularly practised on Sundays in Lent by the young sons of the citizens. Members of the King's household, and of the retinues of bishops, and many other people, came to watch. During the Easter holidays the boys played at a sort of naval battle. A shield was fixed to a tree by the river. Then a boy stood with a lance on the high stern of a boat which was

122

Boys' game – quintain

rowed as fast as it could go downstream. The game was to strike the shield and break the lance. If the boy missed, or did not break the lance, he fell into the water. Just beyond the shield two boats were moored to pick up the unlucky or unskilful ones, while people crowded the bridge and the upper rooms of houses to applaud or laugh.

At the horse fair there was always racing, and another writer tells how all the earls, barons, knights, and citizens came to the fair to see the horses and watch the racing. The jockeys were boys, trained for the sport, though no doubt this was business rather than sport to them, and winning horses sold for better prices. No mention is made of betting, but there was always gambling, and it is hard to believe of so English a sport as horse-racing there was not the equally English practice of betting.

Another amusement was the quintain. A shield was fastened to one end of a long pole, and a bag of flour to the other, and the pole was pivoted on another upright pole. Either on a horse or on someone else's back the player charged the shield with a lance, and had to dodge the bag of flour as it swung round on the impact.

These were not the only amusements practised by boys. The rules of conduct for the boys of Westminster school lay it down that when going to church they shall *not* run, or skip, or chatter, or fight, or carry a bow, or a staff, or a stone in the hand, or anything by which someone might be hurt. In the dormitory they shall *not* tear their companions' beds to pieces, nor hide the bedclothes, nor throw shoes or pillows from one corner of the room to the other, nor, to sum up, rouse anger or throw the whole school into disorder. There were no playgrounds, nor, with the general view of childhood, was it likely that anyone should think them necessary. Children played in the streets, which no doubt, then as now, pleased them very well, though there was the danger of being run down by a horseman. A favourite playground, not intended for that purpose, was St Paul's Cathedral, then, and until the Fire of London, a magnificent Gothic cathedral in the heart of the city. As a church it was greatly misused, and a letter survives written by Bishop Braybrooke in 1385, complaining, among many other things, that a lot of good-for-nothing boys throw and shoot stones, arrows, and other missiles at the birds nesting in the walls and porches of the church. They also play ball inside and outside the church, breaking the stained-glass windows and the painted stone images of the saints. In the fourteenth century the tide of hooliganism washed much higher up around the piers of decency and order than they do today.

How many boys went to school it is impossible to say. Conditions varied very widely. In the country quite tiny children were set to work at jobs that were within their range, like bird-scaring. At the same time, even a remote country village might have a priest who would teach promising little boys their letters. By this means even the son of a serf might have his feet set on a ladder which could lead him to the highest places in the kingdom. Such seems to have been the career of Bishop Wykeham, or, in the fifteenth century, Bishop Waynflete, coming from the Lincolnshire village of that name, who founded the colleges of Eton, and Magdalen, Oxford. The chances of such a rare combination of great ability, ambitious

Books and the rod at school

or tolerant parents, a good primary schooling, a patron to support the boy through Oxford or Cambridge, and the luck of health and further patronage, were of necessity very rare. Yet there must have been fairly numerous little schools, run by the village priest, or, in a small town, by a chantry-priest or by some old woman, or schools attached to the cathedrals and larger churches where there were choirboys who had to read in order to sing the services. By the middle of the fifteenth century perhaps as many as half the total population could read English—which partly explains the desire to have the Bible in English. The most popular book in the fifteenth century was Nicholas Love's *Mirror of the Blessed Life of Jesus Christ*. In Chaucer's lifetime there must have been many people who could read and were starved of the pious reading matter they desired. At these elementary schools, or song schools as they were called when they were attached to a cathedral church, children were taught to say Our Father and Hail Mary, the Creed, the Ten Commandments, the Seven Deadly Sins, and a few psalms, all in English. It can be seen that no concessions were made to the infant understanding, though probably few children were set to this learning before the age of seven. There were no books graded in difficulty, no stories specially written to appeal to the special interests of the child. No wonder everyone in the fourteenth century says that school was hated. On the other hand the remorselessly religious and moral nature of the education obviously had a very powerful effect. We cannot be surprised that practically all men of any education, especially when that education was so powerfully reinforced by the general habit and thought of the age, turned sooner or later, or off and on, to the Church, whatever their sins and cynicism in the full flush of life. This is as true of Chaucer who, in the end, astonishingly as it sometimes seems to us, condemned all his writings that were not specifically religious, as it is of the exceptionally brutal and unpleasant John Holland, Richard's half-brother, who made a pious pilgrimage. There are a hundred instances of piety besides all sorts of wickedness in men's lives, which tempt us to simplify their motives and natures and call them simply insincere, cynical, or hypocritical. Perhaps some of them were. Yet to be human is to be inconsistent. When we suspect deliberate hypocrisy, we should remember how men were forced into this educational mould, and how different were the other forces of lawlessness and competition, that worked upon them. And though we may deplore such educational rigidity, it at least gave some sense of security and a noble scale of values.

A knight's or nobleman's son would not go to a song school. He had as a tutor some chaplain, or, if he were of really exalted family, like the Black Prince, some well-known scholar. Song schools and their like were for the middle and poorer classes of society, and were usually taught by chantry-priests or other clerics.

The little boy who is described so charmingly in Chaucer's *Prioress's Tale* is the only son of a poor widow, who is attending school because he is a choirboy. On the other hand it is possible that Chaucer himself attended or had some connection with a song school. The most important of the three London grammar schools in Chaucer's time was that of St Paul's Cathedral, and attached to this grammar school was a song school. About the middle of the century this song school had an unusual schoolmaster, William Ravenstone, who had a large collection of books in Latin. Although he was a chaplain, he seems to have had very few theological books, but a great many other books of various interest, including some practical teaching books and a large number of Latin classics. When he died he left these books to the school, to the number of eighty-four, and with them a chest to keep them in, and provision for an annual gift of money to the boys. To feel the full significance of this one must realise the extreme booklessness of the fourteenth century. There are some 76,000 wills surviving from the fourteenth and fifteenth centuries in England. Of these Miss Deanesly examined 7,568, and found only 388 which bequeath books; yet this was a period when books were valuable and so likely to be mentioned in wills. The wills containing books are far fewer in the fourteenth than in the fifteenth century, and usually only one or two books are mentioned in each will. So Ravenstone's eighty-four are really outstanding. Furthermore, it was extremely difficult to get the use of a library. Most of those that existed were in monasteries, and restricted to the use of monks. On the other hand, Chaucer himself from an early period shows a quite unusual knowledge of the classics, while his parents' house was not far from the song school of St Paul's. So it is possible that Chaucer got his unusual knowledge from Ravenstone's collection, and that the learned and kindly Ravenstone may have been Chaucer's own teacher, either at the song school, or retained as a private tutor by Chaucer's father. We cannot be sure, because there is not enough evidence and the possibilities are almost endless; but not a few men of educated tastes can look back to an unusually good schoolmaster for the first fostering, if not the first awakening, of their special interests, and for lending or pointing out the books which are at the basis of a lifetime's reading. Although it was so bookless an age, Chaucer himself, like most poets, was an extraordinarily well-read man, and himself owned, he tells us, sixty books, which again is a very high number for the times. It may be that we have William Ravenstone to thank in some small but not unimportant measure for Chaucer's knowledge and love of books, and so for much of his achievement.

Books were scarce because they were so toilsome to produce. Printing in England was still almost a hundred years away. Paper was slowly coming into use, but the skin of sheep or calf was still

A library

Scribe at work

the usual material of books, and the supply was short and the preparation elaborate. Ink and pens were not easily to be bought: the ink had to be made up, and the quill-pens cut from a goose's feather. Scribes sometimes complain about the quality of the pen, or the paper, or the cold of the cloister, in the margins of the books. Serious literature was still almost entirely in Latin, contained in huge tomes which included many separate items. One book might constitute almost a small library. Each item was written in folded sheets, like a pamphlet, which were then bound together to form the large book. Sometimes discoloured sheets in a book show that one of the pamphlets which make it up was left for a long time before being bound up with others, and its outer page had become dirty. Scribes wrote on sloping desks, with a stick in one hand to hold the page steady without smudging it, and pen in the other. Most writing was still done in the monasteries, but stationers are recorded in England from the beginning of the century, and by the middle of the century there may have been a commercial bookshop in London. It was probably the only one in England, though Florence had several. The London shop may have employed as many as half a dozen scribes, who busily copied out various items which were then bound together. Professional scriveners, who copied out books for people, are recorded from the middle of the century, and probably existed before. They often made mistakes, and a good many scribes seem to have left mistakes uncorrected even when they noticed them, because a correction spoiled the look of the page. For this reason a beautiful manuscript may be less reliable in its text than a manuscript untidily written out by a careful amateur. One is bound to make mistakes when copying out by hand. None of Chaucer's own manuscripts survive, but those of his Italian contemporary, Boccaccio, are still preserved, and he made plenty of mistakes when copying out his own poetry. Each copy will have variations, which become complicated when you have copies of copies. All manuscripts are different, all are corrupt, though some less than others. That is why the reconstruction of Chaucer's or Langland's text is a highly technical and laborious job, when, as in the case of *Piers Plowman* or *The Canterbury Tales*, up to eighty manuscripts have to be taken into account and compared. Chaucer at the end of *Troilus* shows his anxiety about the preservation of a correct text, and soon after he finished *Troilus* wrote an amusingly irritable little poem to Adam his scribe:

> Adam scriveyn, if ever it thee bifalle
> Boece or Troylus for to wryten newe,
> Under thy long lokkes thou most have the scalle   *scab*
> But after my making thou wryte more trewe;
>   *unless according to what I have written*
> So ofte a daye I mot thy werk renewe,   *I must renew thy work*
> It to correcte and eek to rub and scrape;
> And al is thorugh thy negligence and rape.   *haste*

A good example of the sort of book an educated man might have is provided by the Thornton Manuscript, now at Lincoln Cathedral. It was written about the second quarter of the fifteenth century probably by a country gentleman, Robert Thornton, who became lord of East Newton in Yorkshire in 1418. He wrote a rather similar book (now British Museum manuscript Additional 31042) and probably these two miscellanies were all his books, and served a variety of purposes. The Lincoln manuscript contains a prose life of Alexander, translated from the Latin, followed by the lamentation of a sinner in purgatory, followed by the alliterative poem *Morte Arthure* which is one of the group of alliterative poems to which *Sir Gawain and the Green Knight* belongs, and was composed in Chaucer's lifetime. Then follow several rhymed romances, a life of St Christopher in couplets, a tale of the miraculous conversion of a wicked knight through a miracle of the Virgin Mary, followed immediately by a rather improper funny story, more romances, more religious verse and prayers in great quantity, religious tracts and sermons, and finally a collection of medical receipts. There are over seventy separate items, comprising history, romance, religion and medicine. It is a very fair indication of the taste of an educated person of the late fourteenth and the fifteenth centuries, and in type, if not in quality, represents tastes very similar to Chaucer's.

The Thornton Manuscript is written in a rather careless, unformed hand, in the ugly Gothic script of the fourteenth and fifteenth centuries. It has little decoration. Most manuscripts, like most books today, had little adornment, and were much less beautiful than most books are today. Even so, they were very expensive when professionally produced. The cheapest, of only a few leaves, cost about a shilling, which must be multiplied at least sixty times to find its equivalent today. Few good books cost less than ten shillings then, and standard works of philosophy etc., of the kind of which Chaucer's Clerk had twenty by his bed, cost two to three pounds. No wonder his overcoat was threadbare. The book that the Wife of Bath threw into the fire, because her young husband read to her stories unfavourable to women from it, must have cost one to two pounds. Splendidly decorated books cost a very great deal more, since they might mean the employment of several skilled men for several years, although naturally in all these cases the costs varied greatly with the books and the conditions of sale.

All this shows that Ravenstone's bequest of books to his school was generous both in literary riches and in sheer economic value.

It seems likely, from the terms of his will, that whether or not Ravenstone was Chaucer's teacher, he taught more Latin than was usual at a song school. The place where Latin was chiefly learnt was the grammar school—hence its name. The whole body of European learning, except the most elementary, was in Latin, and in order to enter the world of learning, or even of professional administration, it was necessary to learn Latin. Up to the middle of the century, as I have already said, it was usual to construe the Latin into French, thereby, it was hoped, killing two birds with one stone, but very often, one would imagine, missing both. Chaucer knew French very well, possibly through this method, or because they spoke French at home, or because he had a special tutor. At any rate, Chaucer knew French better than Latin, and was always glad to use a French crib if he could whenever he undertook any translations from Latin, just as he used a French crib, recently discovered by the researches of Mr Pratt, to help him translate the Italian of Boccaccio's *Il Filostrato*. At the grammar school pupils entered the first part of the general Arts course, which was called the Trivium, consisting of Rhetoric (the art of speaking), Dialectic (the art of logical argument), and Grammar, which included not only learning grammar, but all the business of understanding authors, and all that would now go under the headings of literary history and criticism. But primarily it meant learning grammar. Again we have to remember the difficulty of getting books. Often, even at the university, a lecturer would simply read out a book sentence by sentence, and the pupils would copy it down and learn it by heart. Often in learning grammar they simply learnt off by heart the standard textbook in Latin verse or prose. It is no wonder that village priests, who might have spent only a year or two at the university, often after a few years really knew no Latin at all. It is not surprising that the general standards of Latin were extraordinarily variable, and often scandalously low (though there was only one bishop in the fourteenth century who was so illiterate he couldn't read. He was the Black Prince's nominee, Robert Stretton, and the King forced his election as bishop against the opposition of the Archbishop of Canterbury).

When a boy went to a grammar school, what was his aim, or his parents' aim for him? That the impassioned pursuit of knowledge for the sake of understanding was as strong then as now we are bound to believe, if only from Chaucer's portrait of the Clerk of Oxford. It is the noblest portrayal of that ideal anywhere in English literature, and wonderfully free from the embarrassment that tinges all later attempts by English writers to describe an ideal of learning that any man might be proud to follow. It is not likely, however, that the pursuit of pure knowledge was any stronger then than now, and the general opinion was perhaps even less in favour of it. All learning, and especially Theology, the Queen of the Sciences, as it was called, was useful learning, to save souls, to administer the law, to cure the sick. And the three professions of the Church, law, and medicine were in fact the likely aim of anyone who entered a grammar school at least up to the time of Chaucer. Latin was the foundation of all three. Moreover, the practitioners of all three professions were usually what it is now convenient to call clerics, that is to say, members of one or other of the official ranks of the Church, though not necessarily priests.

The reason for this is that when the ancient world went under to the barbarians, in the fifth and sixth centuries A.D., it was the Christian Church which alone preserved in the West what learning and civilisation there was. In the Dark Ages, with very few exceptions, only churchmen could read or write. The whole story of the European mind from the sixth to the sixteenth centuries may be summed up as the attempt, against appalling difficulties, to preserve, to re-discover, and to extend the learning of the classical world of Greece and Rome. The so-called Renaissance of the fifteenth and sixteenth centuries is really not a rebirth but the most triumphal stage of that process. In Italy, where continuity was strongest (and leaving out of consideration the Arab and Byzantine worlds, which for long preserved more than was granted to the West), there may always have been a few laymen who could read and write. But to the bar-barian nations of the north of Europe, including the English, it was Christianity itself which brought knowledge of words along with the Word. And both were in Latin. A cleric (the word itself is Latin), or clerk, was a minister of the Church, and so inevitably, because Christianity is the religion of the Book, he was one who could read. And still, at the end of the fourteenth century, to be able to read was in itself regarded as evidence that a man belonged to the official ranks of the Church. This could be an important privilege, for if accused of a serious crime such a man might demand to be tried by canon law rather than by the law of the land, and canon law was often more lenient. If a man were convicted of murder, he would hang by the ordinary law. But if he could claim 'Benefit of Clergy' he received a lighter punishment. And he proved his 'clergy', which meant both his learning and his clerical status, by showing he could read Latin. It is characteristic of medieval admin-istration that this test of being able to read became stereotyped; it was usually the highly appropriate first verse of the fifty-first psalm (fiftieth in the Vulgate) beginning 'Have mercy upon me, O God'. (One wonders how many illiterates learnt this off by heart.) It came to be known as the 'neck-verse'. The last man of any note to claim Benefit of Clergy to escape the penalty for murder was the Eliza-bethan playwright, Ben Jonson.

The second half of the fourteenth century saw the beginnings of

important developments in education. It saw the coming into existence of literate laymen, men who could read not only English but
Latin, and who could probably write it at a pinch. The prime
example of the new literacy is Chaucer himself. Another is Gower,
who composed poetry in English, French, and Latin. Henry IV
knew Latin. None of these could or would claim to be in minor
clerical orders. Most of the knights and ladies of Richard's court
could read English. Many of them, at least until right at the end of
the century, could read and speak French, though probably with a
provincial English accent, while the translation of a stanza from a
well-known Latin schoolbook in Chaucer's poem *The Parliament of
Fowls* suggests that at any rate some of the courtly audience would
have been expected to remember their Latin schooling.

We do not know if Chaucer went to a grammar school, or if he
had a private tutor. Perhaps there was not so much difference; most
schools had little more than half a dozen pupils at a time. Naturally
London was different, but even that was a small city by modern
standards, and with a terribly high death-rate. Few places can have
swarmed with children, and most children must have grown up in
small groups, even at school, ignorant of the huge tribes we are now
familiar with.

In all this the discussion has centred on boys; what of the education of girls? There seems to have been no prejudice against women
getting what education they could, but on the other hand, no one,
including women themselves, seems to have made much provision
for their formal education. Convents occasionally took in girls as
boarders, where they were taught deportment and manners, and
also, if necessary, a little reading, but it would have been rare indeed
to find a woman who could read Latin. The place of women in
late fourteenth-century society in England is indeed something of a
mystery. From Chaucer's poems, and what we hear of such ladies
as Joan of Kent and Alice Perrers, it is obvious that they occupied an

important though ill-defined position, even in political matters; but the documentary evidence is lacking. A number of poems (mostly, it is true, of the fifteenth century) claim to have been written by women, but in most cases a man is clearly the author. Yet just over the Channel there flourished the poetess and dauntless lady, Christine de Pisane, who after her husband's death when she was twenty-three maintained herself and her three children in courtly circles by her poetry, which is not among the least of its age. Such a woman is exceptional anywhere, at any time, but perhaps the courts of France and Burgundy were more favourable to such a chance than was that of England. Even Chaucer, after all, seems never to have been able to maintain himself by his poetry, though no doubt it helped; he worked hard as a courtier. Gower was a small landed proprietor. Langland scraped a miserable living praying at funerals for the souls of the dead.

Women of all ranks got their education where they could, now in a song school with their brothers, now in a convent, now from a tutor or their mother. As Bartholomew, following Aristotle, notes, and it is still true, girls are more pliant, docile, quick to learn than boys, and many a sister has benefited from lessons intended for her brother, like Maggie Tulliver in *The Mill on the Floss*. In the thirteenth-century romance *Floris and Blaunchflower* the boy will only go to school if the girl goes too, and so she is sent. But she had not been meant to go originally.

Whatever education women may have had, there was no special provision for them in grammar schools, and from grammar schools on, therefore, it is only a question of men's education. And the men who were educated were only a small proportion of the whole, though how small one cannot tell. Probably one man in five was some kind of a cleric, and therefore at least minimally educated. Perhaps we might reasonably double this twenty per cent, which included many doctors and lawyers, to include the children of the upper classes and of tradesmen and of such few peasants who could or would receive some learning. What further education was available to this part of the population after it left grammar school somewhere around the age of fifteen?

The first thing we notice is what a sharp break existed between being a 'child', and being grown up. At one moment boys were being treated as children, under strict government, and then they were to all intents and purposes treated as men. There were no stages in between, no idea of adolescence. In 1360 all 'men' between sixteen and sixty were required to prepare themselves for war. Possibly some of the violence, irresponsibility and touchiness of fourteenth-century Englishmen was due to this abrupt change.

The state of the universities would certainly bear this out. The early records of Cambridge were mostly destroyed, so our evidence comes chiefly from Oxford, but this does not matter so much, since Oxford was the more important of the two English universities of the century. At the beginning of the century it was probably the best university in Europe, especially for mathematics and science and certain kinds of philosophy, but after the middle of the century it may have declined. Its chief faculties were theology and medicine and law, but before proceeding to such studies everyone went through the general training of the Arts course, composed of the Trivium already mentioned, and the Quadrivium, which was made up of music, geometry, arithmetic and astronomy. There is no need to go into detail here about university studies and life, because there are many good discussions of the subject, and because Chaucer himself did not go to the university. It will be enough to say that many grammar-school boys did go to the university. They might for a time continue a grammar-school type of course, which was necessary, since the usual age of entry was about fifteen. If they were going to be priests they might spend only a year or two at the university, or at least not stop to take a degree. If they wished to become men of learning the course was very long, and might not be finished until they were thirty, or even much older. If they went so far they might hope for a university position themselves, or for employment by some great man, or by the King, as administrators or diplomats. They were educated by lectures, and also by taking part in formal arguments, called disputations. Medieval universities were intellectually very lively places, as was Oxford until crushed for Lollardy by Archbishop Courtenay in 1382. Almost every kind of heresy was put forward; every kind of subtle argument, including of course some foolish ones, was indulged, and recantations were frequent. Until 1382 Oxford was genuinely the intellectual power-house of the country, as a university ought to be. It was also extremely riotous, as may be imagined from the large numbers of boys and young men suddenly released from strict discipline into such a free and boldly argumentative society. There were some six

A university lecture

or seven colleges, and apart from the innovation of Wykeham's New College, these colleges had few undergraduates. The vast majority lived in halls, which were really no more than lodging-houses containing some dozen or twenty students, under the charge of 'regents' who were Masters of Arts, and themselves for the most part young men in their middle twenties. Other students lived in ordinary lodgings, like the Nicholas of Chaucer's *The Miller's Tale*. The lively behaviour of the student in this tale, and the other two Cambridge students in *The Reeve's Tale*, is a fair index of the behaviour of many of these not altogether suitable candidates for the learned and sober professions.

At Oxford there was violent hostility between the Welsh and the North and South Nations, that is, between those who came from those various parts of the country; and also between Town and Gown. The riots that arose were often led by quite senior members of the university. The chronicler Adam of Usk tells rather coyly how in 1388-9 there was continual trouble between the Welsh and the northern nations, in which he was a ringleader of the Welsh. In 1388 he says that the Northerners were driven right out of the university. In the next year they returned in force and besieged the Welsh in their halls, breaking into and plundering some of the halls, and killing some of the Welsh students. On the third day the Welsh found reinforcements from Merton Hall, and there was a battle in the public streets, which the Northerners had made their camp. The King's judge had to descend to punish and make peace. But the most famous riot of all was the 'Great Slaughter' of St Scholastica's day, 10th February 1355. Here the worst violence was committed by the citizens and men of the surrounding countryside, who on two successive days broke into the halls and killed sixty-five students. 'Gown' was driven right out of the city, and the King had to punish the townsfolk heavily. The Mayor of Oxford still did annual penance for it in a procession to the university church right up to the nineteenth century. The quarrel was founded on the enmity caused by the citizens' loss of rights to the university, but it was sparked off by the rough behaviour of some students. They went to a tavern at Carfax, disliked the wine, and said so. The vintner replied sharply, and the students threw the pot of wine at his head. Within a little while the bell of St Martin's Church was calling the citizens to arms, and the bell of St Mary's, the university church, was sounding, by the chancellor's orders, to call out the university. This particular occasion was outstanding because of the damage and loss of life, but minor incidents of violence were always common. The chancellor of England in 1377, for example, was Adam Houghton, Bishop of St David's, who was born not far from there. Forty years before his appointment, when an Oxford student, he was in trouble for wounding another clerk and his wife. So it was not only arguments that were violent, as dozens of illustrations could show. In the Lollard controversies, one of the disputants on the orthodox side (which was not popular in the university) lost his nerve when he saw, or thought he saw, that twelve of his listeners held weapons concealed under their robes. He believed that death was threatening him unless he got down from the chair in which, according to custom, he was maintaining in public his argument. Yet against such rowdiness we should balance the intense zeal for intellectual matters which in a rather odd way it bears witness to. Especially we should remember the solid, essentially quiet, laborious, disinterested work of the mind, which was carried on by many of those scholars who never appeared in law-court reports; which in all its purity and nobility has been caught for all time by Chaucer's portrait of the Clerk of Oxford, with his sober manners and thread-bare coat, who would so gladly either teach or learn. We might also notice that with his special interest in the philosophy of Aris-totle, he was as likely as not a scientist. The word 'philosophy', until the nineteenth century, included what we now call 'science'.

A fourteenth-century astrolabe

Although Chaucer did not go to Oxford, in one way at least he was unquestionably linked to Oxford thought, and in other ways he may well have been profoundly influenced by it. The certain influence is in science, in particular, astronomy. He wrote *The Astrolabe* and quite possibly *The Equatorie of the Planetis*, and these are both products of the Merton school of mathematics and astronomy that flourished especially in Oxford in the middle of the century. (In that he wrote these works in English he is also a remarkable pioneer in his own right.) Chaucer must have known Oxford men about the King's court, and it is possible that the Strode to whom, with Gower, the *Troilus* is dedicated, was a Merton man—there was certainly a fellow of Merton of that name. At Oxford again, in the earlier part of the fourteenth century, there was a new interest in the Latin classics. The best-known person in this revival of letters is the famous book-lover and collector Richard de Bury, Bishop of Durham, who died in 1345, and of whose treatise *Of the Love of Books* (*Philobiblon*) at least twenty-eight manuscripts survive. He was a man such as the schoolmaster Ravenstone, who must also have been educated in a university. Chaucer himself, and all reading men of his generation, benefited from the Oxford enthusiasm for Latin literature and from the new commentaries that were made. There was also a tremendous surge of interest in the first half of the fourteenth century in Oxford in the study of logic, and with it, culminating in Ockham, an altogether new scepticism. The English passion for logic was famous. It led to the testing of many accepted assertions, and, in Ockham, to an almost complete separation of faith from reason. This spirit spread among the upper classes, and Langland speaks bitterly of how great men on the dais in hall would irreverently discuss the most sacred and difficult mysteries of the Trinity. Chaucer's own scepticism must surely have taken something from this Oxford-born element of the spirit of the age, as well as from his own inborn flippancy. There is a notable example of such scepticism in his most typically courtly poem, *The Knight's Tale*, where he makes the Knight say of Arcite's death,

> His spirit chaunged hous and wente ther,
> As I cam nevere, I kan nat tellen wher.
> Therfore I stynte, I nam no divinistre: *am no theologian*
> Of soules fynde I nat in this registre.   *account*
>
> *The Knight's Tale, CT* I, ll. 2809-12

On the other hand, the divorce between faith and reason did not lessen men's devoutness, though it may have made it less rational. Chaucer himself wrote plenty of devotional literature in prose and verse. There was an increasing spirit of lay devotion, shown in such treatises as Henry of Lancaster's *Livre de Seyntz Medicines*, and John Clanvowe's treatise which will be mentioned later. It was connected with the universities through such movements as Lollardy, which is associated with Wycliffe, the most controversial schoolman of the late fourteenth century (who was for a time at Merton). And one of the most important things about Lollardy was its attempt, however crude, by laymen, and in the English language, to bring faith and reason together again. The new spirit of lay devotion was part of the new assertion of the importance of the English tongue. Whether Wycliffe himself wrote the many sermons and tracts in English once attributed to him, is now thought to be doubtful, but their association with him is significant enough. This new vernacular movement grew partly out of men's ignorance of Latin even in the university. When the Archbishop had notices condemning Lollard doctrines posted in Oxford in 1382, he had them written in both Latin and English. This can only mean that he thought they might not be understood in Latin. Chaucer's labours in translating from Latin the immense sermon that is *The Parson's Tale* suggests that there was as well a positive demand for religious writing in the vernacular by people who in former years would have been content with their ignorance. Towards the end of the century laymen not only demanded religious writing in English, they demanded the Bible. Some of them even wrote religious treatises in English. Whereas Henry of Lancaster wrote in French, Sir John Clanvowe, the Lollard knight, who probably wrote the Chaucerian poem *The Cuckoo and the Nightingale*, also wrote in English the sermon preserved in a manuscript now at University College, Oxford. So the movements of mind in Oxford in the early and middle parts of the century spread throughout English literary culture, through books, and also through the Oxford clerks, who became parsons, confessors, lawyers and administrators throughout the land.

The universities were not the only destination open to a grammar school boy, though they were much the most usual. The son of rich parents might also go to one of the Inns of Chancery and Court. This has a special interest because it is a reasonable guess, though unfortunately little more than a guess, that Chaucer himself attended one of these Inns. For seven years, from 1360 to 1367, there is no record of Chaucer, though before that we know that he was in a great household; while it is not unlikely, in view of his later career, that he had some knowledge of the law. What is suggested is that he was possibly a part-time student of the law during this period, as we know other men to have been who were esquires of the King, or who held similar positions in other great households. Not only those who intended to make a career of the Common Law went to these Inns; the sons of rich men who would inherit large estates found the training useful; and careers very like Chaucer's, in government, were beginning to open out for men with this sort of training and the necessary social background (which was not a requirement at the university). For full-time study it was usual to enter an Inn of Chancery at about the age of sixteen, and then after a couple of years to go on to an Inn of Court, such as the Inner Temple. The education was expensive, but more than purely intellectual; students were supposed to be taught singing, dancing, noble games, and noble manners. They were also expected to read the Bible and to read chronicles. It was the contemporary idea, in fact, of a liberal education, the education of a gentleman.

The young gentlemen in these Inns were as lively (to use no harsher word) as young gentlemen in any other age. There is a record from 1325, printed by Miss Rickert, of a characteristic student brawl in London in which a man was killed, the students in this case being 'apprentices of the Bench', that is, law students from the Inns of Court. There is also a tradition that Chaucer as a young law student was fined for beating a friar in Fleet Street.

Whether or not Chaucer ever was a student of law, it is certain that he was first a page in the great house of the Countess Elizabeth of Ulster, who was married to one of the King's sons, Lionel. The earliest record of this comes from 1357, when he may have been seventeen, but was probably nearer thirteen. This was the age at which Christine de Pisane's son first entered the household of Sir John Montague, third Earl of Salisbury, as mentioned earlier. After the seven years silence in the records of Chaucer's life we find him first a 'valectus' and then an esquire of the King's court, which shows him to have moved up the rungs of advancement from page onwards, but remaining in very much the same sort of environment. In fact, the traditional education for a boy or young man of good birth who wished to enter courtly circles was provided by making him a page in some great household. It went back to the ancient Anglo-Saxon and Germanic practice of 'fostering' a young noble in the retinue of a king or lord, and it continued until the sixteenth or seventeenth centuries. One might almost say that the public schools took over the same function.

Much of such education was 'education by living'. To observe the manners of the great, to hear or talk to great men, and, not least, great ladies, to pick up the inner gossip of the ruling circles, all this, for a lively and observant boy, must have been an incomparable preparation for the life of a courtier. There may even have been a certain amount of formal instruction from a chaplain in book-learning, and from the master-at-arms in the management of weapons, armour, and horses. To judge from the early fifteenth-century courtesy books, however, the principal emphasis was on manners, on 'courtesy', the usage of courts. Courtesy came from heaven, says one of these books, when the angel Gabriel greeted Our Lady, and all virtues are contained in it. Then the instructions carry on in the next line—see that your hands and nails are clean, don't start eating until grace is said, and so on. These fifteenth-century books probably make the whole business more external, more efficient, more moralistic, more bourgeois, than it can have been in practice. There is little doubt that pages and esquires picked up plenty of bad habits as well as good, and the life itself in Edward's court must have given them a good deal more sophistication than is suggested by the worthy fifteenth-century clerks, with their passion for conformity and efficiency, who wrote the handbooks that have survived. Yet no doubt the handbooks give much in the way of emphasis and organisation that was characteristic of the fourteenth-century court. Russell's *Book of Nurture* has been quoted. Another interesting one is *The Boke of Curtasye* in the British Museum manuscript Sloane 1986, of the early fifteenth century.[1]

When you come to the lord's gate, says the writer, give up your weapon, and ask leave to go in to speak to whomever you wish. If it is a person of low degree you want to speak to, he will be fetched. If a gentleman or lady, then you must go to him or her. When you get to the hall door take off your hood and gloves. If a meal is in progress when you go in, greet the steward, controller and treasurer (officials of the household), bow to the gentlemen on each side, take notice of the yeomen, and stand in front of the screen at the back of the hall by the entrance until the marshal or usher (whose job it was to put people in their places according to their rank) leads you to your place. The setting can best be imagined as like that of the hall of an Oxford or Cambridge college today, with a dais at one end, at which sat the important people, including the officials, and long tables down the hall where sat, in order according to rank, the gentlemen, yeomen, and followers and servants of lower degree, the lowest nearest the door. Then, the book goes on, when you are

[1] In *The Babees Boke*, ed. F. J. Furnivall, Early English Text Society, O.S. 32, 1868.

placed, if you are among the gentlemen, be steady of behaviour, polite, and don't talk much. Cut your bread the right way, have your nails clean, be pleasant, don't argue or make faces, don't cram your mouth with food or eat noisily; don't leave your spoon in the dish, but clean it. This instruction in table-manners was a common-place in such manuals. Another writer translating from Latin adds don't drop food on your chest, don't snatch after your food; another says don't dip your food too deep in the sauce, and keep your lips clean. Several books say dry your mouth before you drink. Chaucer clearly knew such instructions from what he says of the Prioress in the *General Prologue* where his description gives them life:

At mete wel ytaught was she with alle:	*meals*
She leet no morsel from hir lippes falle,	
Ne wette hir fyngres in hir sauce depe:	
Wel koude she carie a morsel and wel kepe	
That no drope ne fille upon hire brest.	
In curteisie was set ful muchel hir lest.	*desire*
Hir over-lippe wyped she so clene	*upper lip*
That in hir coppe ther was no ferthyng sene	*tiny part*
Of grece, whan she dronken hadde hir draughte.	
Ful semely after hir mete she raughte.	*food*
And sikerly she was of greet desport,	*was very cheerful*
And ful plesaunt, and amyable of port,	*friendly in manner*
And peyned hire to countrefete cheere	*imitate*
Of court, and to been estatlich of manere. . . .	*dignified*

General Prologue, CT I, ll. 127-40

This is just as much reminiscent of the manuals as it is of a passage in *Le Roman de la Rose*. But the effect here is rather to suggest that the Prioress has *learnt* these manners, that they don't come naturally to her. The word 'curteisie' used in this passage is significant, when we remember such a title as *The Boke of Curtasye*. Though 'countre-fete' simply means 'imitate', without the idea of producing a worthless copy, it seems clear that Chaucer is mocking the Prioress, as he might have mocked, without fundamentally disagreeing with, the authors of the courtesy manuals.

The Boke of Curtasye, however, goes on with further details which Chaucer spares us. For example, you must not spit over or on the table—that would be uncourteous. Don't scratch your dog while eating—an especially necessary instruction when people helped themselves to food with their hands. You may use the table-cloth as a napkin. If you blow your nose, wipe your hand discreetly on your skirt, or on your cape 'that is so gay'. Handkerchiefs were little used. The chroniclers comment on the fact that King Richard used one; and it suggests the fastidiously aesthetic strain in his character.

After a section of the usual good advice to children, *The Boke of Curtasye* gives an account of the various duties of the officials of the household. It would be too long to go into them all, but we might just pause to look at the functions of the grooms of the chamber, since this was one of Chaucer's early positions. The groom makes up the beds, which are of straw, and nine feet long and seven feet broad. A lord has two beds, an inner and outer, with various hangings, counterpane, cushions, and a carpet. The groom also looks after the fuel, screens, tables, trestles, and benches, warm water for ladies, wax candles to be set over the chimney-piece. When such offices had to be done for a king they were much sought after, and it is clear that those who performed them needed to be well trained. Among other instructions there is set out an elaborate ceremonial for washing the hands. In Edward IV's court in the later fifteenth century, which is thought to have preserved much earlier customs, it was twelve knights, and valiant men of that order, who were responsible for 'serving the king with his basin' to wash in. All this was done with great deference, the grooms kneeling before the person who was to be served.

The instruction in such ceremonial as this was at the core of the courtly education of the later Middle Ages, not only in England but also in other courts, where, as in fifteenth-century Burgundy, it reached far more elaborate extremes. It is not to be despised, nor is such discipline as merely external as it seems. As famous regiments have found, it is the rigid parade-ground drill, carried to what seems to the outsider fanatical extremes, harsh and mindless in itself, which inculcates that general discipline and powerful *esprit de corps* which can resist all but the most violent attacks and changes. The loyalty which a system like this creates is not so much towards a person as towards an institution, a regiment or a court, and it combines efficiency with conservatism. This particular institution, the court, seen as an administrative machine, was the creation of Edward III, his ministers, and a number of barely known devoted officials, as well as of the 'spirit of the age'. The French knights mocked it, and what they no doubt thought was the pettifogging spirit of accountancy and bourgeois manners within it. But the court survived the senility of Edward, the extravagance of Richard, the change to Henry, and the Wars of the Roses; the system of education, and all that it demanded, from keeping the nails clean to keeping the accounts straight, was surely the ballast which enabled it to sail through such rough waters. The books of courtesy played their part.

CHAPTER SIX

Court Life

THE court was a mixture of ceremony and practical usefulness in which the one often supported the other. The courtesy books with their emphasis on good manners influenced the way the court actually worked, and the way the court worked affected the nature of the ceremonies and amusements which took place. All the same, there was a distinction between ceremony and amusement on the one side, and practical usefulness on the other, and their distinction is reflected in the records we have. The life of leisure, the fine flower of court culture which is the chief subject of this chapter, had roots in utility. But all too often the records show us only roots or flower and, as in the court game of the Flower and the Leaf, the two often seem in opposition. Our knowledge of Chaucer's life suffers. His poetry is the finest petal in the flower of the court culture, and he was famous in his day even in France. Yet the records show him only as a minor courtier; a diplomatic envoy; a Comptroller of Customs; Clerk of the Works; member of commissions such as that which inquired into the state of the Thames embankments; subject to writs for small debts. What a portrait of England's famous poet! Yet in such details, interesting enough in themselves of course, we must ground ourselves, if we are to recreate in imagination that beautiful but transient flower of court culture that in the fifteenth century so quickly faded and fell. Chaucer knew that

> al nis but a faire
> This world, that passeth soone as floures faire.

It is Vanity Fair that we shall be describing. But we can still take pleasure in it, learn from it still, even from its passing, and we may well think that it is in imagination quite as delightful, quite as useful, and much less harmful, than ever it was in reality.

The King's court was in origin simply the household of the greatest of the 'magnates' or great lords. There were vast estates to be administered, rents and debts to be collected, justice to be done, a thousand daily decisions large and small to be taken. All magnates had such big households, comprising all ranks from the humblest kitchen-helper to the magnate's personal council, which in John of Gaunt's case was a hundred and fifty strong. But the King's household was now something more than that of the greatest magnate; it was turning into the administrative centre of the kingdom. Originally domestic departments, like that of the wardrobe, were also departments of government. The wardrobe became divided into the King's wardrobe, the great wardrobe, and the privy wardrobe. The great wardrobe became as it were the Ministry of Supply. The privy wardrobe became an armaments store, settled in the Tower of London, where it was responsible for stocks of bows and arrows, pikes, lances, equipment for horses, tools, and even that new material which was to destroy knighthood, gunpowder. Departments such as these were becoming detached from the court proper, but their dependence on it was still close. The same is true for other departments of the king's government, such as the law-courts. The King had been the chief law-giver, but he no longer sat on the bench of justice. Parliament had grown out of the council of great men who advised the King, though it was also a court of law, but the developments of the century, notably the King's need of money from the nation for the nation's wars, which he could not finance out of his own estates, forced him to make Parliament more representative of the nation at large. Members of Parliament, judges, heads of great departments of state, were many of them courtiers also; so, in his minor way, was Chaucer, Justice of the Peace, and in one Parliament a knight of the shire for Kent.

The court itself, and all these various parts or aspects of it, had at the beginning of the century no fixed place of abode. One reason was that such large gatherings of people were difficult to feed at a time when communications were slow and almost every household had to be self-sufficient. The court had to move about the country so as to spread the burden of its maintenance. This was the case not only for the King's court but for the court of any magnate, or even sometimes for the abbot of a great monastery. This ceaseless activity was still characteristic of the King's court right to the end of the century. When Froissart paid his last visit to England, in the middle thirteen-nineties, he says he stayed in the King's court as long as he pleased, not always in one place, for the King often moved to Eltham, to Leeds, to Kingston, to Sheen, to Chertsey, or to Windsor, all of them in the surroundings of London.

It had been necessary for the King's court to move not only to find provisions, but to govern the country, and all the departments of state moved with him. Even in the late fourteenth century Parliament met in different places, such as Gloucester and Northampton, as well as at Westminster. But the important development of the latter part of the century was the increasing fixity of the departments of state at Westminster, and their consequent detachment from the King and his court. They began to have a life of their own, which increased their efficiency, but which also altered both their character and the character of the court. The court became rather more a place of entertainment and less a place of business.

As a result, it was possible to realise the essential courtly life more fully than in any previous English court. From the time at least of Richard's marriage to Anne of Bohemia in 1382 a great court existed for the first time in England, taking much of its inspiration from the papal court of Avignon and the French court at Paris. It was leisured though still basically functional; it had many people (far too many, in the opinion of Parliament); most of these people were on a footing of general equality; there were many ladies, decorative, distracting, and, some would say, inspiring; a number of patrons and patronesses of the arts of life and the life of Art.

New demands for luxuries imported from the South, new feelings about the way life should be lived, new feelings about literature, paintings, music, were all seeping in from the southern courts, to settle in the poetry of Chaucer, based so largely on French and Italian poets of the new movements, like Machaut and Boccaccio. If one major influence which Chaucer felt and recorded was the new mixture of devoutness and scepticism, mathematics and morals, the other major influence was the new decorativeness, new concreteness, new sensibility, which characterise the court-culture of his time.

It is not easy for us to imagine the type of establishment with which the King was surrounded, and which made up his court. Richard's own court is too big to be described, but a suggestion of the elaborate organisation and multifarious activities of such a court can very well be gained from a few extracts from the registers of the Black Prince, who in his day was the flower of princes. These records of payments, administrative decisions and the like open up many windows on the times. Thus there is a long list of payments made on 5th September 1355. The sums paid are not important, but the totals of which they are part show how a medieval prince valued what he thought important or desirable. An embroiderer of Brussels is owed £1,436 8s. 4d.; Martin Parde of Pistoia, a jewel merchant, £3,133 13s. 4d.; a London goldsmith £574 3s. 8d.; another embroiderer £295 4s. 10d.; yet another of Cologne £97 15s. 11d.; Hugh le Peyntour of London is paid for painting £82 13s.; John Parde of Pistoia, a jewel merchant, is owed £242; Lambkeyn, a saddler of Germany, is given an advance of £1,368 for saddlery for a forthcoming campaign. Various knights also receive payments. Here is evidence, like that of Chaucer's poems, for the international quality of the court-culture of the day. Another long list of pay-

ments was made on 7th July 1361. It is an order to the account of
Sir Peter de Lacy, the Prince's clerk and receiver-general, to allow
the said Sir Peter over £2,000 to make a number of payments.
Some of them are sums without any comment, which are presumably retaining fees for members of the prince's council, or other
members of his court, but there are others as well as knights to be
paid. Willyn the piper receives £11 13s. 4d.; Cok the farrier receives 13s. 4d.; Sir Emenynyou de Pomers, £100; the messenger from
La Rochelle, £8 6s. 8d.; Jakelyn the piper, £16 13s. 4d.; Raulyn
the Prince's falconer, £6 13s. 4d.; seven of the Prince's minstrels
receive a gift in the Prince's chamber of £9 6s. 8d.; a horse given
away costs 13s. 4d.; a falcon, not given away, 66s. 8d.; Sir Lewis
Clifford as his fee for last year gets £20; Hugh le Peyntour is paid
again, and William Ivot, goldsmith, receives a payment. The jewel-
ler from Pistoia, the embroiderer from Brussels are paid again, and
money-lenders receive something on account. Several knights receive instalments of sums of £100 or more which the Prince promised them for their services at the battle of Poitiers. It is easy to
see here the 'magnificence' which men expected of a prince; and
also the efficient administration which maintained the courts of magnates and the King. Such payments are not quite typical of the
register as a whole; the entries are almost daily, and the prince did
not spend hundreds of pounds daily on jewellery; the usual run of
entries refers to the continual stream of minor decisions, judgements
and payments connected with the running of a great estate, and
though the Prince himself often ordered them, high officials, trusted
knights of his household, did most of the administration, or advised
the Prince.

Another example of court life is offered by the establishment
which the captured French King John kept, when he moved to
Lincolnshire. He had to dismiss forty-two of his attendants, keeping
about the same number with him. He had two chaplains, a secre-

The courtly game of chess

tary, a clerk of the chapel, a doctor, a *maître d'hôtel*, three pages, four valets, three wardrobe men, three furriers, six grooms, two cooks, a fruiterer, a spiceman, a barber, a washer, a chief minstrel (who also made musical instruments and clocks) and a fool or jester. He also had with him Philip, one of his sons, who had been captured at the same battle; for himself, his son, and the fool he fitted up a room each with hangings, curtains, cushions, ornamented chests, etc., each roomful occupying the space of an entire wagon when he moved. Wines, spices, sugar (he was extremely fond of sweets) were imported or bought on a large scale, over and above the normal necessities of life. He also bought a great number of suits of robes at huge expense, and provided generously for his household in the same way. One of his robes, trimmed with fur, took 2,550 skins. His time seems to have been spent reading romances and playing music, chess, and backgammon. His son was more interested in hunting-dogs, falcons, and game-cocks. John was noted for his generosity, that truly medieval virtue of kings. Wherever he was he made a daily offering to the curate of the parish, and gave large sums at festivals of the Church. The orders of friars were favourites with him, as they were with all the members of the upper classes except authors, and he gave them much money. Here is court life in little: its luxurious extravagance, flowing with a stream of beautiful and colourful personal possessions—furred clothes, gold and silver enamelled cups, painted and carved chests, rich tapestries—and in generous gifts; idleness, dallying with fiction, music, indoor and outdoor games; and a sincere, devout, limited Christian devotion.

Idleness, or at any rate leisure, is necessary to the attainment of any way of life that is not merely governed by brute necessity. John, however, suffered from enforced idleness, as the English court did not. Much of the decorative part of court life served practical purposes, even political purposes, while the performance of practical necessities was enlivened by turning them into occasions for ceremony and enjoyment. Some feeling of this underlay the justification of such a life. Why should lords and prelates be allowed more delicate foods, clothes, etc., than ordinary men, asks the monk and scholar, Uthred of Boldon, and immediately proceeds to answer himself: because, according to Aristotle, superiors are occupied with the mental and spiritual work of government, while others are occupied with less demanding bodily work; and superiors are more discreet in avoiding excess, and so may be allowed more subtle food and so on, while subjects are less able to restrain themselves. But illicit self-indulgence is even less lawful for superiors than for inferiors. The working of such feelings of justification in practice are seen again in the case of King John. He returned to France, leaving hostages, including his son, for his ransom; these hostages broke their parole and returned to France. Deeply humiliated, the King insisted on returning to prison in England, against all the advice of his nobles. Here was a fine sense of that truth and honour which for Chaucer distinguish the Knight, besides the generosity and courtesy which are equally a part of the ideal, and which John had also amply shown. The justification for such a life, in fact, lies in the ideal of chivalry, an ideal which Richard himself, at the end of his life, claimed he had always followed.

The age of chivalry was always in the past. Every age when the ideal was current saw how miserably it was upheld. Yet all knights

at least paid it lip-service and often it must have softened and en-
nobled lives otherwise thoughtless and harsh. Chivalry eventually
produced in England one of the most potent ideals of social behaviour that the world has drawn from the West—the ideal of the
gentleman. Probably we are seeing, or have already seen, the last
age of this ideal, but it still deserves honour. In the fourteenth
century it was still maturing, but yet Chaucer conveys much of its
essence in his portrait of the Knight in the *General Prologue* to *The
Canterbury Tales*.

Chivalry was the code of the knighthood, the armed retainers of
great lords, the most important fighting men, who were drawn from
the upper classes of society. Since the prime need for any society is
to maintain itself, and this can ultimately be done only by force, in
the days when force depended largely on personal strength the chief
persons in society were those best able to fight by force of arms. In
an age without technology the mounted horseman was supreme.
Chivalry began in the eleventh century when these rough and violent
men began to be brought to recognise some of the medieval Christian
ideals. It developed with the polishing of manners which a slowly
improving civilisation made possible, and which borrowed much
from the superior civilisation of the Arabs, with whom the West
fought so long, especially in Spain. The improvement in manners
led to a special conception of love which it is not too much to say is
the tap-root of our whole idea of romantic love. Personal bravery,
Christian faith, polished manners, love: these are the elements of the
chivalric ideal—an ideal confined, of course, to the knightly class,
strictly inappropriate to clerics and peasants.

In the life of the Black Prince by Chandos Herald, which was
quoted in Chapter Three, the two chivalric virtues which are emphasised are bravery and loyalty; and with them go *franchise*, generosity, and pity. In *Sir Gawain and the Green Knight* the virtues of
the hero, Gawain, are *franchise*, fellowship, chastity, courtesy and

pity. The bravery that men admired was, in our eyes, sometimes a foolhardy recklessness. Sir Ralph Hastings did not value death at two cherries, says Chandos Herald, and Sir William Felton 'the valiant, very boldly and bravely charged among the enemy like a man devoid of sense and discretion'.

The loyalty was usually conceived on an intensely personal level. It might be loyalty to one's lord, though the lower ranks of the people seem to have felt this more than the upper. It might be loyalty to one's friend. We have almost lost the concept of the passionate friendship between men that is part of the basis of *The Knight's Tale*, and which was quite free from perversion. It is said that when Sir John Clanvowe died abroad in 1391, his friend Sir William Neville, another of the Lollard knights, died within two days of grief. It is curious that the feeling for this kind of attachment has almost completely dropped out of our literature. Another type of loyalty, which has probably swallowed up the type just mentioned, is that of the knight for his lady.

Franchise means a manner of well-bred ease and naturalness. It implies self-confidence, and therefore a frank and easy approach to other people. Pity is a virtue obvious in itself; Chandos Herald says that the Black Prince undertook the Spanish campaign out of pity and friendship for the exiled King Peter. One of Chaucer's favourite lines (which he probably took from Italian poetry) is

For pitee renneth soone in gentil herte   *runs; noble*
  The Knight's Tale, CT I, l. 1761, *The Merchant's Tale*, CT IV,
  l. 1986, *The Squire's Tale*, CT V, l. 479, *Prologue F, The Legend
  of Good Women*, l. 503; cf. *The Man of Law's Tale*, CT II, l. 660

Pity is the virtue that Chaucer most often expresses. It had its limitations; Chandos Herald does not tell us, but Froissart does, of the sack of Limoges, when the Black Prince looked on unmoved as men, women, and children were slaughtered on their knees as they besought mercy from the English soldiers. His stern heart was at last melted when he saw three Frenchmen gallantly and desperately defending themselves against a greater number of Englishmen. These fighters he spared.

Generosity again is a self-explanatory virtue, yet even so it had somewhat different aspects. A knight was expected to be without regard for money and possessions:

> Fy on possessioun   *Fie*
> But if a man be vertuous withal!
>
> *CT* V, ll. 686-7

says Chaucer's Franklin. Generosity was especially the virtue of a prince, and Edward III and the Black Prince were both models of knighthood in the prodigal way in which they scattered rich gifts among their retainers and friends. Men loved the prince to be magnificent and if he had not been he would have lost their regard. As a result, the treasuries of medieval kings were continually in trouble; Edward bankrupted several great Italian banking houses, simply by not paying what he owed them, and though the Black Prince had enormous revenues he died heavily in debt. On the other side of the picture it was becoming increasingly possible to make one's fortune at court, and men like Clanvowe, Burley, Stury, and even Chaucer himself, must obviously have been in a sense on the look-out for personal gain.

The last virtue was courtesy. In this had once been included all the others, but by the end of the fourteenth century its chief meaning was 'good manners' of the kind that was encouraged by the courtesy books already mentioned. Perhaps the extreme of the new delicacy of manners that was being slowly developed was Richard's use of the handkerchief. An earlier example is the Black Prince's insistence on serving King John as a squire after the King had been captured at Poitiers. Courtesy was conceived very much in terms of speech. The knightly and learned educations both emphasised the 'art of speech', which Chaucer refers to, for example, in *The Squire's Tale*. Ability to speak convincingly was continually needed in the courts of law, in diplomacy, in university disputations, in the King's court; but as well as usefulness a grace was sought. Thus when Sir Gawain reaches the castle, and people learn that he is the Gawain of Arthur's who is famed for his courtesy—'Lo, Gawain with his olde courtesie' as Chaucer elsewhere describes him—they rejoice that he will be able to instruct them in the 'stainless terms of noble speech'. Chaucer's perfect knight

> nevere yet no vileynye ne sayde
> In al his lyf unto no maner wight.   *to any kind of person*

And in *The Book of the Duchess* the Black Knight does not fail to praise the *eloquence* of his lady.

The ideal was not staid. Time and again there is emphasis on joy as one of the supreme qualities or even virtues of courtly knights and ladies. Joy is not so appropriate on the battlefield, though most knights loved fighting. The traditional praise is 'like a lion on the field', but it goes on, 'like a lamb in the hall'. Joy was especially the virtue and the reward of lovers. Chaucer says at the end of the third book of the *Troilus* that he has 'said fully in his song'

> Th'effect and joie of Troilus servise.

In the portrait of the lady in *The Book of the Duchess*, which is almost wholly taken from French sources, the lady's gaiety is everywhere praised, and, though care is taken not to make her appear lightminded, 'dulnesse was of hir adrad'. Nothing is more typical of the courtly ideal than the praise of joy; life was so often nasty, brutish and short; youth passed soon; religion was often gloomy and repressive, but even if, as in one of Chaucer's favourite phrases, 'ever the latter end of joy is woe', then at least let joy be gathered while it flowered.

The contrast between the chivalric courtly ideals and an aristocracy without these ideals is well shown by a curious narration of Froissart's. He reports the experiences of an English knight who had been captured by the Irish, spent seven years among them, married the daughter of his captor, and eventually returned to England, where he was useful in the court as an interpreter of Irish. After Richard's first Irish expedition four Irish kings swore obedience to the English king, and he wished to make them knights. The English knight was appointed to improve their manners, and told Froissart (I give a shortened version):

The King gave them first a very handsome house in the city of Dublin for themselves and attendants, where I was ordered to reside with them. I observed that as they sat at table, they made grimaces that did not seem to me graceful, and I resolved to make them drop that custom. When these kings were seated at table, and the first dish served, they would make their minstrels and principal servants sit beside them, and eat from their plates and drink from their cups. They told me this was a praiseworthy custom in their country, where everything was common but the bed. I permitted this to be done for three days; but on the fourth I ordered the tables to be laid out and covered properly, placing the four kings at an upper table, the minstrels at another below, and the servants lower still. . . .

They had another custom I knew to be common in the country, which was the not wearing breeches. I had, in consequence, plenty of breeches made of linen and cloth, which I gave to the kings and their attendants, and accustomed them to wear them. I took away many rude articles, as well in their dress as other things, and had great difficulty at the first to induce them to wear robes of silken cloth, trimmed with squirrel skin or miniver, for the kings only wrapped themselves up in an Irish cloak. In riding they used neither saddles nor stirrups, and I had some trouble to make them conform in this respect to English manners.

I once made inquiry concerning their faith, but they seemed so much displeased, I was forced to silence. . . . (However, they believed in God and the Trinity, and, there being two warring Popes at the time, they fortunately, like the English, inclined to the Pope who was in Rome.)

The King wished to create these kings knights, and the Earl of Ormond talked to them of the order of knighthood they were to receive, explaining to them every article and ceremony of it, and how great a value should be set upon it, and how those who were created knights should behave. . . . They were made knights by the hand of the King of England, on the feast of Our Lady in March, in the cathedral of Dublin. The four kings watched all the Wednesday night in the cathedral; and on the morrow, after Mass, they were created knights, with much ceremony. . . . The four kings were richly dressed, suitably to their rank, and that day dined at the table of King Richard, where they were much stared at by the lords and those present.

The English knight speaks in some ways like a nineteenth-century missionary, with a heartening faith in the rightness of English manners, if with more caution in the matter of religion. He brings out well the ideal and social qualities of chivalry, and the genuineness with which it was accepted. He suggests the elaborate ceremonies connected with the giving of knighthood, and its religious basis, emphasised by the all-night vigil in the church. He reveals once again the hierarchical structure, the insistence on higher and lower, of courtly society, and the concern with proper clothing.

The remark about how everybody stared is a reminder that courtly society, though in ideal and often in practice, with all its bowing and kneeling, very much more ceremonious than ours, was also in many ways surprisingly free and easy. This is partly because of the gulf between theory and practice, never more apparent in English society than in the Middle Ages; but it is also a genuine expression of the nature of the court. Although Richard in his later years liked to bully elderly prelates and make them kneel before him, he allowed his bodyguard of Cheshire archers considerable freedom with him—'Dickon [i.e. Richard] sleep safe while we wake,' they said in their dialect, following this with a broad joke, which a disapproving chronicler quotes. It was easy for all sorts of people to get near the King and gaze at him while he ate. There were court fools, who were allowed to behave wildly. Clanvowe in his religious treatise says that the fool has a 'bauble', with which he beats people, and is often beaten in turn. Great lords, in their passion, could behave wildly to the King. The extravagance with which the feelings of knights and others are expressed in literature is therefore in large part a genuine reflection on the way people behaved, which has been mentioned in an earlier chapter. The lovers' madness of *heroes*, which the young men in *The Knight's Tale* suffer, was something recognisable in life, even in medical handbooks. When Malory, in the fifteenth century, says that Queen Guinivere laughed so much at a joke that she fell down, it is not an absurd exaggeration.

The chivalric and courtly view of life is entirely accepted by Chaucer, and he deepens and ennobles the ideal, while also showing himself occasionally not much interested in some of the more superficial and popular parts of it. In this he shows himself rather similar to Richard, and different from the majority of English people. In the *General Prologue* the knightly ideal is split up between two characters, the Knight and the Squire, his son. The Squire represents the more obviously youthful parts of the ideal, the gaiety and fashionableness of courtly life, the bright clothes, the music and poetry, and the interest in love. The Knight represents the deeper moral qualities of the ideal, which the Squire has yet to grow into.

The Knight

> loved chivalrie,
> Trouthe and honour, fredom and curteisie.

'Truth' is one rendering for loyalty, but goes beyond this. It is the supreme virtue of Troilus, and implies not only loyalty but a strong personal integrity. There is a moral deepening and broadening of the ideal here. Just as in Chaucer's use of the word 'honour' in his mature works there is a sense of moral worth deeper than the meaning of 'good reputation', so in his use of 'courtesy' he implies a generally noble, gentle, considerate way of life. The Knight, too, avoids the kind of excess in clothing which preachers condemned among the upper classes, though Chaucer is more indulgent to the Squire, letting him appear 'embroidered as a mead'. Chaucer says of the Knight,

And though that he were worthy, he was wise.

This is the kind of praise that was often given to the character of Duke Henry of Lancaster, one of the best men in all respects of the fourteenth century, but it is a little different from the usual courtly ideal; it means that though he was brave, he wasn't foolhardy, whereas the courtly ideal as expressed by Chandos Herald included a bravery that extended to a suicidal recklessness. Chaucer's Knight is a prudent, hardbitten, devout professional soldier, at the top of his profession, very much as we may imagine Henry of Lancaster and several of Chaucer's friends and acquaintances, like Sir Simon Burley, Sir Lewis Clifford, Sir John Chandos, Sir Stephen Scrope, and others. Most of these were companions in arms of the Black Prince. They were not feudal retainers in the old sense, bound to their lord by ties of land and inheritance, but had freely entered into engagements to serve him (as Chaucer's Knight had with the lord of Palatye) for which they received pay. Even the Black Prince when he went to war drew his pay of 20s. a day. Chaucer's portrait is not only of greater moral beauty than the average contemporary description, it is also more realistic.

The sceptical Chaucer quite rejects the Arthurian myth which in England especially was the basis for much of the ceremonial and ideal of chivalry. A Round Table was first held in England in the late twelfth century, and King Richard the Lionheart had actually made a present of 'Arthur's' sword Excalibur to a foreign king.

The Arthurian legend (which is effectively an invention of the early twelfth century) was taken as the basis of the Order of the Garter. The conservative school of alliterative poetry of the North-west Midlands, which so flourished in Chaucer's day (and is unfortunately so little known in ours) was especially interested, in its old-fashioned patriotic way, in Arthur and his court. The belief that Arthur was a fully historical figure, and the most glorious of 'English' kings, was firmly held by most Englishmen up to the end of the sixteenth century, and even Milton gives it up with reluctance. Foreigners were sceptical. Chaucer was as cynical as any Frenchman, and his attitude decidedly different from normal English feeling, though he does not go so far as to take the actual name of Arthur in vain. His references to Lancelot, Arthur's chief knight, are flippant. In his tale of a cock and a fox he says:

> This storie is also trewe, I undertake,   *guarantee*
> As is the book of Launcelot de Lake,
> That wommen holde in ful greet reverence.
>
> *The Nun's Priest's Tale, CT* VII, ll. 3211-3

On the whole, the English writers who translated and adapted the French romances that were the favourite light reading of the fourteenth century were more interested in the exciting events of the stories than in the sentiments, which they often cut out. Here again Chaucer differed from most of his countrymen. Although he pays due respect to the public acts of his chivalric characters he is much more interested in their private and personal relationships and feelings, especially those to do with love.

Love was the great medieval theme. In courtly and chivalric circles this meant particularly the love between young men and women, for the most part in their late 'teens. Although the basis of such love is sexual desire, sexual desire and love even in this narrow sense are not quite the same thing. Sexual urges may be indulged without love, and sex in European Christian thought is specifically connected with marriage, and with the continuance of the race. In medieval Europe, among the upper classes, marriage was also often concerned with property, and child-marriages were not uncommon. But love was a highly refined feeling, in which the emphasis was on the emotional relationship with the beloved, on its pains and joys, and on the ennoblement and refinement of character in the man which were both demanded and produced. It was often outside marriage, and though not merely sexual was sometimes adulterous. The theory and the literary development of this idea of love was especially the work of French writers, and from the twelfth century onwards they called this special set of feelings *fine amour*, 'refined love'. Chaucer calls it the 'art and craft of fine loving'; modern scholars often call it 'courtly love'.[1] Chaucer's phrase suggests the elaboration, the 'institutionalisation', of the feeling, which might range from mad infatuation, as in the story of Tristan, to a polite parlour game, taken seriously by neither knight nor lady. The essence of *fine amour* was the extreme respect that was paid to the lady (who was a lady, not just a woman) by the man. In ordinary life even ladies had few legal rights; they had an inferior status; in marriage the husband 'is the head of the wife'. But in love the lady is the dominant person. At first, indeed, in Provence, she was called a goddess, and always, in the love-institution, she was rather like the feudal lord in the social institution of feudalism. Yet, granted the original division between love and marriage, it was the English genius to reconcile them again, as has never been convincingly achieved in Continental literature. In England *fine amour* in literature was hardly ever adulterous. The romantic ideal of love practically always led to marriage, and marriage was often expressed in terms of *fine amour*. Richard's marriages are examples; an even

[1] For a fuller discussion, and references to other works, see *The Parlement of Foulys*, ed. D. S. Brewer, Nelson's Medieval and Renaissance Library, 1961.

clearer example is John of Gaunt's first marriage to Blanche the Duchess, whose untimely death is the subject of Chaucer's *Book of the Duchess*. The Black Knight in the poem, who represents Gaunt, gives a long account of how he turned in early youth to the 'craft of love', how he long loved his lady, what virtues she had, and how at last, after long service on his part, 'She took me in hir governaunce.' That is, she accepted him in marriage.

The characteristic knightly virtues were also those of the lover, and the bravery of a knight in battle was considered to be enhanced if he were in love. Literature is full of examples—Chaucer's Troilus, Malory's knights, the young Squire in the *General Prologue*.

On the other hand, bravery in war is rarely, even in Froissart, connected with love. That wild and gallant soldier, Sir Walter Manny, could make vows of what he would do before returning to his mistress; occasionally other knights, in the presence of ladies, made foolhardy vows, like promising to fight with one eye blindfolded; but the more usual situation seems to be that of the heroic Chandos. He even remained unmarried, and seems to have been entirely a professional soldier, a prudent man, a good general, merciful; but his virtues are nowhere thought to spring from being a lover. The place for such sentiments was the tournament, which in the fourteenth century was itself becoming a game and an art-form.

The virtue of loyalty was fundamental in love. Time and again the knight's loyalty to his lady is stressed. In this case, the interest in literature is in the conflicts between various kinds of loyalty. For example, in the poem of *Sir Gawain and the Green Knight* the lady of the castle attempts to seduce Sir Gawain. His loyalty to ladies is such that he cannot rudely repel her. On the other hand, he must also remain loyal to the ideal of chastity. Part of the sophisticated delight of the poem is the tension between the two demands. In *Troilus*, there is some slight tension between Troilus's duty to Troy, and his duty to Criseyde; but Chaucer does no more than touch on this. His fullest treatment of the problem of loyalty comes in *The Parliament of Fowls*, where three courtly suitors all claim the same beloved. In order to set their claim high they each emphasise their loyalty to the beloved, which implies life-long constancy. But only one of them can marry her. What then of the fate of the others? Are they to 'serve' hopelessly the rest of their lives? This is what they seem to have committed themselves to. Yet again this sort of problem, though it has its relation to life, is not of a kind that can be illustrated from the records of the century.

The other virtues, of pity, *franchise*, courtesy, generosity, all have their obvious applications to the delicacies and duties of *fine amour*, and in literature these virtues are always said to be enhanced by love. In a word, a lover, because he is a lover, becomes a better man. And once again, in all English literature, perhaps in all European literature, it is Chaucer who has described this effect most nobly, in the passage where he describes the heightened nobility of Troilus, when he is in love with Criseyde, at the end of Book III of the *Troilus*:

> In alle nedes, for the townes werre,
> He was, and ay, the first in armes dyght. . . .   *arrayed*
> And this encrees of hardynesse and myght
> Com hym of love, his ladies thank to wynne,
> That altered his spirit so withinne.

> In tyme of trewe, on haukyng wolde he ride,   *truce*
> Or elles honte boor, beer, or lyoun;   *hunt; boar; bear*
> The smale bestes leet he gon biside. . . .   *he let escape*

> And moost of love and vertu was his speche,
> And in despit hadde alle wrecchednesse;
> And douteles, no nede was hym biseche   *there was no need to require him*
> To honouren hem that hadde worthynesse,
> And esen hem that weren in destresse. . . .

168

And though that he be come of blood roial,
Hym liste of pride at no wight for to chace;
                it did not please him to condemn anyone out of pride
Benigne he was to ech in general,
For which he gat hym thank in every place.
Thus wolde Love, yheried be his grace,   *praised*
That Pride, Envye, and Ire, and Avarice
He gan to fle, and everich other vice.   *every*
                    Troilus III, ll. 1772-1806

Who can tell how sentiments like these have affected behaviour in the medieval and later centuries? It is easy to see the places where men fell short of the ideal; the child-marriages, the wife-beating (though this was not common in courtly circles), the adulteries, the illegitimate children, are all occasional realities of the time, but so is that painful struggle out of barbarism which has been the story of Western society since the collapse of the Roman Empire. In that struggle the ideals of chivalry have played a large part.

One of the benefits of chivalry was the improved position of women. The concept of the 'lady' is one of its best achievements. The lady is beautiful, honourable, educated, eloquent at need, kind, and merciful. She still lives in what is entirely a man's world, and most of her virtues are seen as adaptations of those of the knight. Bravery alone is not required of her. She is passive, not expected to love except after long wooing, and then it is not her love she grants, but her 'pity', her 'mercy'. Rarely is there any sense of equality. The lady is either superior, as in love, or inferior, as in marriage. But her qualified, temporary, and often unrealistic superiority unquestionably affected the rough military society and softened and subtilised it. Many of Chaucer's remarks in his poems show that he was conscious of the ladies in his audience, and no doubt their presence encouraged his interest in the personal and private aspects of life, as a female audience always does—witness the history of the novel, which has always relied on women readers for its steady audience. The typically public and impersonal subjects of literature have until recently interested mainly masculine audiences, and where Chaucer deals with such serious subjects directly and explicitly, as in his writings on philosophy, astronomy, and religion, his audience is not essentially courtly.

The ideal of the courtly life was gay, young, passionate, and colourful. Tournaments, dancing, feasts, these are the joys of the court, to which one must add, as is clear from the poetry, hunting, May games, indoor games, and poetry itself.

The tournament is the best known and most glamorous of these amusements. In the thirteenth century it had been evolved from a frightful mêlée, in which two bands of knights fought each other fiercely (though usually with blunted weapons), to a more orderly affair, in which smaller groups, or only two knights, fought each other in an enclosed stadium. It was both practice and substitute for war. Sometimes the English and French knights when a truce was proclaimed would arrange a tournament, and here the joust in its nature of a substitute for real war can be seen. Indeed, when Edward III began the Hundred Years War, the French King challenged him to single combat, to decide the issues at stake. It is typical of Edward, and perhaps of the English in general, that although he loved the tournament dearly, and was good at it, he staved off the challenge, and preferred the more realistic methods of pillaging and burning his adversary's lands. Chaucer's Knight in the *General Prologue* had 'fought for our faith at Tramyssene three times in the lists, and always killed his foe'.

The tournament could be used to decide an issue of politics or law. An accused knight might appeal to the test of arms to defend his honour. The most celebrated example was when Mowbray accused Hereford (later King Henry IV) of treason. Hereford challenged him, and Richard appointed them to fight it out at a tournament at Coventry, which, as everyone knows from Shakespeare's

A royal banquet

play, *Richard II*, he cancelled at the very last minute. Sometimes
people accused or accusing at Parliament offered to prove the truth
with their bodies. When Brembre, the London grocer and capital-
ist, was accused by the lords appellant, he offered to prove his
innocence by battle 'as a knight should'. The gages (gauntlets and
such) of those who wished to take up his challenge were hurled to
the floor like a hail of snow, but politics intervened, and in the end,
though the King had spoken for him, he was miserably executed.
Sir Simon Burley, in the same crisis, also made the same offer, though
just as unsuccessfully. The Savoy knight, Sir Oton de Grandson,
'flower of them that make [i.e. write poetry] in France', as Chaucer
calls him, lost his life, when quite an old man, in a tournament that

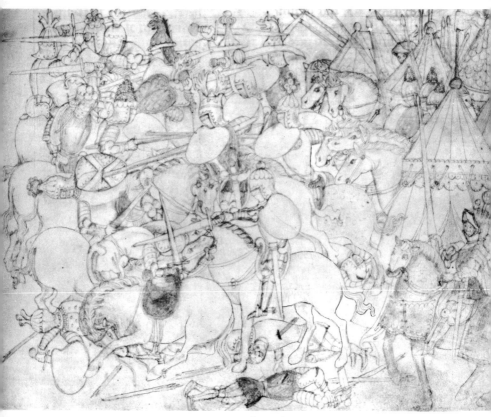

The mêlée

was a judicial duel. In the fourteenth century, however, the tournament also developed towards a courtly sport, fulfilling something of the same function as a modern football or baseball match. The old mêlée was still at least fresh in memory, and in Chaucer's *Knight's Tale* the great tournament, though held within a stadium, or lists, seems to have been of this kind. There were also single jousts, in which two knights hurled themselves against each other and tried to knock each other off with heavy spears, some sixteen feet long. If the spears broke they might continue the fight with swords until one or other was unhorsed. Sometimes the fight continued on foot, until one of the knights was disarmed or beaten down, but towards the end of the century, when the tournament was far advanced towards a sport, the contest seems most often to have been limited to a fight on horseback. Even so it was dangerous enough; in the *Livre de Seyntz Medicines* Henry of Lancaster says you can tell a man who has been in tournaments by the way his nose is knocked about. There are plenty of cases of knights being fatally wounded, even if accidentally, and then the survivor often thought it best to flee, in case he should be imprisoned as a criminal.

This mixture of practical necessity and decorative formal amusement or sport is typical of the court-culture of Chaucer's day. Sir Simon Burley, for example, was an important if enigmatic political figure, and we don't think of him in connection with sports, but when he died there was among his possessions a suit of tilting armour, rather as a set of golf clubs might be among the possessions of a politician today. Like all sport the tournament performed useful social functions. It used up excess energy; it provided a meeting ground for people of various interests (for the common people who watched as well as the aristocracy who took part); it enabled ladies to take part in social life; in a word it was a 'unifying institution', that helped to give a centre and stability to social life. It also helped to contain and work off men's natural pugnacity, which else might have broken out in brawls which in any case were too frequent. Practically everyone rejoiced in the tournament. Langland takes the tournament as the imaginative base for the greatest episode of *Piers Plowman*, when Christ comes to the Crucifixion as a knight to the tournament, dressed in the armour of human nature. In the fifteenth century writers continued to describe the tournament, and it remained a popular entertainment up to the time of Elizabeth I.

A few were less interested, or even hostile to tournaments. The Church, though it eventually allowed them, was always uneasy about them, and preachers often condemned them. More inter-

ivuer uier / au roi qui ne ment mie

Unhorsed!

esting are those who were simply less in love with the tournament, and among these were probably Richard and Chaucer himself. Richard's lack of enthusiasm was noticed, and blamed on the bad influence of his favourites, although he sometimes took part in tournaments. It is obviously unfortunate for any English monarch not to be keen on sport; for a medieval monarch it was disastrous. Richard preferred peace to war, art and poetry to violent exercise, drinking late at night to getting up early to hunt, and these tastes helped to estrange him from his subjects. It was extremely tactless and very typical of him to cancel the great tourney at Coventry between Hereford and Mowbray at the last moment.

Chaucer was not so tactless or lacking in sympathy. In so far as the tournament was part of the chivalric and courtly ideal he accepted and respected it. The description of the tournament in *The Knight's Tale* is wonderfully vivid. Yet the tournament occupies very little of his poetry, whereas it occupied a great deal of ordinary court life.

The most famous tournament in England in Chaucer's time was the great jousting held in Smithfield in 1390. Chaucer did not turn his back on this, for he was Clerk of the King's Works at the time, and was responsible for putting up the scaffolding; but he left no description. Froissart tells us about it. Sixty knights awaited the challenges of all comers, and sixty ladies 'freshly apparelled' kept them company. Heralds had published the festival throughout England, Scotland, Germany, Flanders, Brabant, Hainault, and France, and a number of foreign knights came. It began about three in the afternoon of Sunday, 2nd October, when sixty squires of honour rode sixty war-horses out of the Tower of London. Then followed sixty ladies, richly dressed, riding side-saddle (a fashion said to have been brought to England by Richard's Queen Anne) and each lady leading with a silver chain a knight armed in tilting armour. Accompanied by many trumpeters and minstrels, they rode through the city to Smithfield, where the King and Queen and many ladies waited in richly decorated rooms. The ladies with the knights then took their places with the spectators, the knights were mounted and had their helmets laced on, and the jousting began, continuing till it was too dark to see. Prizes were given, and they all had supper at the Bishop of London's palace, where the King and Queen were staying, and the 'goodly dancing' continued till it was day.

On the next day, says Froissart, you could see many squires and attendants of the knights going about London with armour, and doing other business. This reminds one of the much more vivid passage in *The Knight's Tale* about the lords on their coursers, squires nailing the spears, buckling the helms, putting straps on the shields; armourers bustling to and fro with file and hammer; yeomen and common people going about with their thick staves; and everyone speculating on the chances of the champions. In his description of the fighting Chaucer says that when Theseus decides that the tournament shall be fought with blunted weapons, to save the loss of noble life, the people praise him (a detail which he took from Boccaccio) but it seems more likely that the usual sentiments of the crowd were more bloodthirsty.

To return to the jousts of Smithfield. It is difficult to say if they were in the form of an old-fashioned mêlée, or if the knights jousted separately. Possibly there was a kind of compromise, with a number of single combats taking place simultaneously. On the second day Richard himself led the home party, though he won no prize. Later in the week the Order of the Garter was offered to the visiting Count d'Ostervant, much to the annoyance of the French knights, who thought he was being seduced from his loyalty to France. This seems a likely enough attempt on the part of the English to turn the occasion to political advantage. It was as normal and natural as making business contacts in golf club-houses or at Masonic dinners. The jousting and the feasting continued throughout the week, and finished up with splendid entertainments at Windsor over the week-end.

It is a pity that even Froissart gives us no indication of the details of the feasts. As to Chaucer, he says of such festivities,

> The mynstralcye, the service at the feeste,
> The grete yiftes to the meeste and leeste   *gifts; most i.e. greatest*
> The riche array of Theseus paleys,
> Ne who sat first ne last upon the deys   *dais*
> What ladies fairest been or best daunsynge,
> Or which of hem kan dauncen best and synge,
> Ne who moost felyngly speketh of love;
> What haukes sitten on the perche above,
> What houndes liggen on the floor adoun—   *lie*
> Of al this make I now no mencioun.
>
> *The Knight's Tale, CT* I, ll. 2197-206

This is a neat way of having the best of both worlds. He gives us a little more of such detail in *The Squire's Tale*, where he talks again of the minstrelsy, the dancing, and the love-looking, suggesting in a few lines the whole atmosphere of splendour, the lights, the colours, the gay noise of musical dancing, the undercurrents of personal feel-

ings.   Henry of Lancaster says he often jousted and danced with evil
intent, though such activities are not necessarily evil in themselves.
The *Gawain*-poet describes King Arthur's court in terms of his own
day:

> This King lay at Camelot upon Christmas
> With many lovely lords, knights of the best,
> To reckon of the Round Table all those rich brethren,
> With rich revel aright, and carefree joys.
> There tourneyed knights by times full many,
> Jousted full jollily these gentle knights,
> Then went to the court, caroles to make:
> For there the feast was the same full fifteen days,
> With all the meat and the mirth that men could devise;
> Such noise and glee, glorious to hear,
> Delightful din upon day, dancing at nights;
> All was happiness in the height in halls and chambers,
> With lords and ladies, as most delightful seemed.
> With all the delight in the world they dwelt there together,
> The most famous knights under Christ himself,
> And the loveliest ladies that ever life had,
> And he the comeliest king that the court held;
> For all was this fair folk in their first age, in hall.

ll. 36-55

Towards the end of his reign these delights in Richard's court
must have been something less than perfect, for a chronicler tells us
that he used to have a throne set high up in the hall in which the
courtiers were disporting themselves, and watch them all.   Any
man who caught his eye had to kneel.   But when he was young,
especially in the lifetime of the mild and sweet Anne, feasts must
have come much nearer the ideal.

Music is one of the most frequently mentioned parts of such
feasts and of courtly life in general.   Chaucer several times says how
'heavenly' music is, and this was not a time when the word 'heavenly'

177

'The merry organ' (*CT* VII, 2851)

had been debased into modish feminine slang. The *Gawain*-poet says that the hearts of hearers of music at a banquet are raised full high. All educated people seem to have had some ability at music, though medieval music was so difficult to read that they must always have played and sung by ear alone. There are frequent references in Chaucer's poetry to ladies playing music, while the Squire was singing or playing the flute all day. And not only was the Squire a beautifully dressed young man, and a good soldier and jouster; not only could he write and draw, he could also compose poetry and write the music to it. This was the normal courtly ideal, as we see from several knights and squires in Chaucer's poetry, and also from what we know of such a man as the third Earl of Salisbury. Richard himself wrote songs, though none of them have survived. That great soldier and courtier, Henry of Lancaster, says that from his lips have come many love-songs which have often drawn him and others to sin. Chaucer makes the same confession at the end of *The Canterbury Tales*. One of the noticeable things about the

General Prologue is the number of times music, and particularly singing, is mentioned in connection with the characters, from the Squire
and Friar to the Summoner and Pardoner, and going down to the
Miller, who with his bagpipes led the pilgrims out of town.

Apart from the general ability in music the country was full of
professional musicians, the minstrels. Every lord kept a number of
minstrels on his payroll, as we have seen the Black Prince did, and
their status rose steadily until at the end of the century they formed
their own gilds and elected a 'king'. On the Continent they had
what can only be called Summer Schools, or refresher courses, at
which to improve their art, but there is no evidence of this in
England. On the other hand, music was not their only activity.
King John's minstrel was also a clock-maker. They may also have
recited poetry, but this was probably mostly done by men called
'disours'. The lower type of minstrel, who was not retained by a
great lord, wandered about the country performing all sorts of entertainment, some of it pretty low. The serious-minded Langland
thinks poorly of minstrels, on the whole. It is easy to see how such
a class could reach low depths of vulgar bohemianism, especially
among the lower classes. Their vulgarity might extend to all classes,
however. What may or may not be said in public varies a good
deal at various times—we have seen some astonishing changes even
in our own day in England. In the Middle Ages, for example, all
classes, high and low, appear to have been set off into fits of laughter
at the breaking of wind. It was a subject enjoyed by courtly circles,
as we see from Chaucer's *The Summoner's Tale*. Stories and actions
connected with this innocently unsavoury subject seem to have been
high on the minstrels' and 'disours'' repertoire.

The most regular function of the better class of minstrels was to
play music for meals and at dancing. We have already seen something of the gross splendour of the food itself at courtly meals, but
the food was only part of the feast. The band 'played in' the

courses, just as the bands of various regiments of the army 'play in' the food and accompany the eating on regimental Mess Nights. The favourite music was drums and trumpets:

> Then the first course came with trilling of trumpets,
> With many a banner full bright that thereby hung.
> Noise of new nakers with the noble pipes,   *kettle-drums*
> Wild warbles and strong wakened the echoes,
> That many a heart full high heaved at their touches.
>
> *Sir Gawain*, ll. 116–20

Music was not the only diversion. There were the 'subtleties' already mentioned, and other elaborate table decorations. Chaucer must have been at many elaborate feasts, but this is what he says about them in *The Parson's Tale*:

> Pride of the table appeareth full often; for certainly, rich men are invited to feasts, and poor folk are put away and rebuked. Also in excess of diverse foods and drinks, and especially such manner of baked-meats and dishmeats burning with wildfire and painted and castled with

Musicians at a feast

paper, and similar waste, so that it is a shame to think of it. And also [Pride appears] in too great preciousness of vessels, and ingenuity of minstrelsy, by which a man is stirred the more to the delights of lust . . . and certainly the delights are so great in this case that one might easily fall by them into deadly sin.

The Parson's Tale, CT X, ll. 443-6

The 'wildfire' seems to have been similar to the lighted brandy on the modern Christmas pudding, except that it was done on a much greater scale. The paper was cut out into various shapes, especially of castles, and then painted. It is well known that great Flemish painters employed their skill on these arts in the fifteenth century, and there can be little doubt that such men as the Black Prince's Hugh le Peyntour were similarly employed in the English court in the fourteenth century. Even Henry Yevele, the architect, whose achievements Mr Harvey has done so much to make clear,[1] the

[1] John H. Harvey, *Henry Yevele*, Batsford, 1944, and *Gothic England*, Batsford, 1947.

(see *House of Fama* 1217 ff.)

181

designer of Richard's hall at Westminster which still stands so nobly, and of much else, may not have thought himself vainly employed designing the decorations and kickshaws for these feasts. Such adornments may have been high in the achievements of the arts, even though they were so ephemeral. The monumental and enduring is not necessarily the best. An unintentional compliment is paid to table decorations by the author of *Sir Gawain*. When Sir Gawain, who has long struggled through the wintry wilderness, at last sees under the blue sky a new castle, shimmering and shining through the bare trees, with a huge wall rising out of a double moat, towers, embrasures, battlements, carved ornaments, chalk-white chimneys, painted pinnacles, it is the height of praise to say

That pared out of paper purely it seemed.

It is possible that even more elaborate devices enlivened the meals, though unfortunately the only direct fourteenth-century evidence comes from France. The devices were known as *entremés*—entertainments that were presented between the courses of banquets. Mrs Loomis has studied one that took place in Paris in 1378, when the French King entertained the Emperor Charles IV.[1] It was really a kind of pantomime or interlude, and the nearest we come to the record of such things in England is the *Gawain*-poet's mention of 'interludes' at Christmas, which however must have been much less sophisticated than the French. At the feast in Paris there were five tables for the noblest guests, who were separated by barriers from the crush of eight hundred knights in the body of the hall. The whole company shared a banquet of three courses, each of ten dishes. When the *entremés* began a ship appeared at the end of the hall, like a real ship in all respects to view, beautifully painted and filled with armed men. It represented with an astonishing degree of realism the ship of the twelfth-century crusader Godfrey of Boulogne, come

[1] *Speculum*, XXXIV, 1959.

Westminster Hall, designed by Henry Yevele, Richard II's Master Mason
Copyright The Times

183

to conquer the city of Jerusalem. Men were hidden inside the ship, and carried by them it 'floated' up the hall to the side of the grand dais, where there was a great model of the city of Jerusalem, with a tower, and the Temple, and walls manned with 'Saracens' appropriately clothed and armed and furnished with banners and pennons. The 'crusaders' attacked in the most realistic manner; although the city was so high that parts reached to the roof of the hall, some of the attacking warriors were hurled down from the ramparts, and when the city was eventually won the remaining 'Saracens' were thrown down after them. Godfrey's banner and others were finally planted in triumph on the walls, and the show was over.

This remarkable display was put on for a propaganda purpose; to encourage the kings to undertake another crusade, and the French were more advanced in this sort of thing than the English. Furthermore, although Froissart says that the English were much more ready to pay taxes than the French, it is not hard to imagine the views of Parliament and of many good administrators on the cost of such a show. Yet even so, the French and English courts were sufficiently alike to make one feel that entertainments of the same kind, if less elaborate, must have been put on in the English court. The English lacked the chroniclers rather than the will for and delight in display. There was a splendid series of pageants that the City of London put on for Richard's visit of reconciliation in 1392. Among the sights, of jewelled courtiers and resplendent aldermen, of fountains running with wine, was a wonderful tower in Cheapside. It hung suspended in the air by ropes. On it stood a youth dressed as an angel, and a beautiful crowned girl. They descended towards Richard and Anne as if walking on air, surrounded by clouds. The angel held a beaker of wine, the girl two gold crowns, which were offered by the warden of the city to the King and Queen. The record of all this is in Latin in a poem by Richard Maidstone, John of Gaunt's friar confessor. If the city could put on a show like this, surely the court could also, when the occasion demanded it. Such shows remind us, too, that ceremonial was not only indulged in for fun. There was often a political reason for the more resplendent ceremonies, if only the desire for political prestige. The outer life represented the inner life, and there was often a clear allegorical or symbolical meaning to outward display.

It is difficult now to penetrate to such significances. There was, for example, the game of the Flower and the Leaf. The chief references are in Chaucer's *Prologue to the Legend of Good Women* and Gower's *Confessio Amantis*, in each case a brief, casual mention, as of something well known to the audience of the poems. How we lack educated courtier-chroniclers such as the French and other nations possessed! It seems, however, that the whole court was divided into two factions, one called the Leaf, and the other the Flower, and they engaged in some sort of debate about love. The fifteenth-century poem entitled *The Flower and the Leaf*[1] suggests something of the nature of such debates, and states the claim of the Leaf to be more enduring than the Flower, but this poem has nothing to do with the actual groupings of the fourteenth-century court. Pretty well all we know about these is that John of Gaunt's daughter, Philippa, was the patroness of the Flower, and that Chaucer says that he himself doesn't belong to either group. It would be surprising, however, if the groupings even of an obviously frivolous and poetical game did not have some sort of political colouring, if only because those who are like-minded and friendly in one set of circumstances are found often to be grouped together in others.

Another ceremonial that we can only guess at was that of St Valentine's Day. In France in the fifteenth century on this day courtiers gathered to sing or declaim their poems before ladies, and there was a game of choosing partners for the coming year. Some-

---

[1] *The Floure and the Leafe*, ed. D. A. Pearsall, Nelson's Medieval and Renaissance Library, 1962.

thing of the same game survived in England until quite late in the nineteenth century, though gradually descending in the social scale, and as everyone knows there are still vestiges of the custom to be found. There are a number of Valentine poems in English that date from the fourteenth century, of which the best known is Chaucer's *Parliament of Fowls*. There can be little doubt that they were part of some sort of ceremony, probably presided over by some great lady. Perhaps, as in France, the best poet was given a prize. Certainly poetry was often public entertainment, or was invoked in aid of public entertainment.

There were other varieties of public entertainments. Stow gives a charming account of a mumming put on, again by the City of London, to entertain Richard when he was a little boy of ten, just before he became King. A great number of men clothed as knights and squires, followed by an 'emperor' and a 'pope', then twenty-four 'cardinals', and, rather oddly, eight or ten 'devils', came to Kennington palace where he lived with his mother, Joan of Kent. They played dice with the little prince, using loaded dice to make sure he would win, and presented him with a ball, a cup, and a ring, all of gold, as well as giving presents to the courtiers. Then they all drank, the minstrels played, and everyone danced, the prince and the lords on one side, the mummers on the other, for a long time.

In May people of all classes went to fetch in the may, the hawthorn flower, and to bring home fresh green branches to decorate the houses. In *The Knight's Tale*, which is so much more realistic than the pretentious poem of Boccaccio on which it is based, one of the heroes goes out to pay his observances to May, and rides out of the court a mile or two

To maken hym a gerland of the greves	*from the groves*
Were it of wodebynde or hawethorn leves,	*honeysuckle*
And loude he song ayeyn the sonne shene:	*under the bright sun*

'May, with alle thy floures and thy grene,
Welcome be thou, faire, fresshe May,
In hope that I som grene gete may.'

The Knight's Tale, CT I, ll. 1507-12

To judge from later accounts the Maying was often not very decorous. Large numbers of people spent the whole night out, and no doubt the Puritans were right in considering it a pagan affair, an opportunity for riot and debauchery. But the courtly Maying was more delicate than simpler country matters and in Chaucer's poetry we feel chiefly the sense of sweetness and relief—the wonderful escape for medieval men from the smoke and drabness and rawness of winter, and the delightful promise of summer's pleasure and richness to come.

The amusements of most men in the court were active and outdoor. Of these hunting was the chief, and the sound of the dogs, the bustle and excitement of gaily-clad riders, the thrills of the chase, the triumphant chanting of the horns, were among their highest joys. Forests were near every town and village, with their game usually preserved for the King or for the lord of the manor. A large literature surrounded the subject, and knights prided themselves on their skill, not only in the chase, but also in the art of butchering the dead animal. Boar and foxes were hunted, but above all the deer, and often the slaughter was heavy, for hunting had the practical utility of providing fresh meat at times when there was none other to be had. Most domestic stock was slaughtered in the autumn, because of the difficulty of winter feeding, and the meat was then eaten or salted down. By the time it had been kept a few months it must have been poor stuff. As we have seen, the poor had little meat at the best of times. When Lent came, 'the crabbed Lenten', there was probably little choice but to go with little or no meat even for the better off. So the hunting in wintertime was not only great fun, it was something of a necessity. The glorification of this in poetry comes in that remarkable poem, *Sir Gawain and the Green Knight*, where the butchering of the deer is dwelt on as lovingly as the chase, and this no doubt represents the usual feelings about the matter. A foreigner who attended one of Richard's hunting parties thought he had never seen so noble and delightful a company. But the chronicler Walsingham tells us that the King's favourites were thought to discourage him from hunting and hawking. Once again the intellectual Chaucer shows himself rather in tune with Richard, and rather out of tune with the usual feelings. We do not find in Chaucer, as we do in Shakespeare, a whole series of images, at most stages in his life, drawn from hunting and the equally favourite sport of hawking. There is only one hunt in his works, in one of his earliest poems, *The Book of the Duchess*, which is vividly described in its opening stages, but which the poet very typically strays away

Hawking

188

from very early, led by the genius of French poetry, one may say (for he uses French poems as his source), to hear the lament of the Black Knight. Nor does hawking interest him much more, though he several times uses birds to represent courtly lovers. Human relationships were his chosen interest, apart from his intellectual concerns.

When it was impossible to be outdoors, people occupied their leisure in talk and dancing and indoor games. The favourite game was chess, and medieval romances have a number of references to this, and similar games. In earlier times this apparently innocuous amusement could end disastrously with one of the players hitting the other over the head with the heavy board, but I know of no such incident in Richard's court. Nor does the game of chess, or any similar game, figure much in Chaucer's work. Once again, the chief example appears in *The Book of the Duchess*, written at a time when Chaucer was most typically a fourteenth-century courtier. Here the game of chess provides a simile for the Black Knight's loss of his lady—a simile, incidentally, which the poet represents himself as failing to understand.

Unfortunately few English chroniclers and historians at any period have shown much interest in the arts, and we are never told that Richard spent much time looking at pictures. Yet he must have been interested. It is to be feared that the chroniclers, if they thought about it at all, would have lumped such an interest in with Richard's other frivolities and effeminacies. Unfortunately, too, most of the artistic products of the reign have perished. Nevertheless, it is clear from the records collected by Mr Harvey that there was a surprisingly large number of artists in London in the latter part of the fourteenth century, and that there was in particular a flourishing court school of painters which matched the variety and energy of the general artistic developments of the time. They make it seem likely that this was a period of quite unusual English achieve-

The Wilton Diptych.

See Note

ment in the visual arts. The great example is the Wilton Diptych. It is a solemn hierarchical piece of work, of extraordinary delicacy and brilliant colour, one of the most beautiful English paintings of any period. It is meant for some solemn purpose, and shows well the combination of decoration and utility, the religious idealism and probably the political deliberation, which are so characteristic of Richard's court. (See the note on p. 202.)

As to the other forms of painting, in books and on glass, they need books, not a few lines, to do them justice. There are still many manuscripts preserved which were decorated, or illuminated, as it is called, at this period. Among the best are the famous East Anglian psalters, such as the Gorleston and Luttrell psalters, and Queen Mary's Psalter, of the early or middle part of the century. They are distinguished by the delicacy and vivacity of their line drawing, and the fresh realism of many of the details. Some of them show comic birds and animals that remind one of Chaucer's *Parliament of Fowls*. Many other manuscripts have colourful decorated borders, though the standard seems to have declined towards the end of the century, and the style became somewhat coarsened. Foreign artists were sometimes employed. Richard had a Bible illuminated by a foreigner, Hermann Scheere. That Bible is now the biggest book in the British Museum, with hundreds of vivid and interesting pictures in it. The manuscript of *Troilus* that is in Corpus Christi College, Cambridge, has a fine frontispiece, already mentioned, that is reproduced as the frontispiece of this book, and the Ellesmere Manuscript of *The Canterbury Tales* has a number of delightful portraits of the Canterbury pilgrims, some of which are also reproduced. All the pictures in this book that are taken from manuscript sources were made in England as far as is known in the middle or late fourteenth century, though they have been chosen for their illustrative rather than their artistic value.

Some very beautiful stained glass was made in the fourteenth

Monkey-bishop addressing
a congregation of ducks

century, though almost all of it has now gone. Some very good examples can be seen in New College Chapel, Oxford. The King's Chapel at St Stephen's, Westminster, burnt down in the nineteenth century, had brilliant glass and wall-painting. Some houses and palaces had stained glass as mentioned earlier, which has not survived, but most of it was in churches.

What we should like most of all to know about in the social life of Richard's court is the way in which literary and intellectual life went on. Chaucer towers over all his contemporaries, but there were many other writers about whom we know all too little. Often they wrote in French and Latin, and this side of the poetic life of the court has received little attention. Unfortunately, much has been lost. Richard's own poems, and the third Earl of Salisbury's poems, are gone with the snows of yesteryear. Most courtiers, like Chaucer's Squire, must have been capable of turning verses, and many of

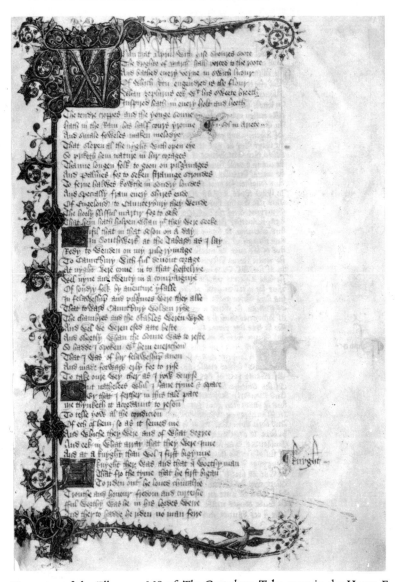

First page of the Ellesmere MS of *The Canterbury Tales*, now in the Henry E.
Huntington Library, California

these would have been in French, though Sir John Clanvowe wrote the best Chaucerian poem that is not by Chaucer in English in the late 1380's. Chandos Herald must be remembered here, though his editors consider him to have been most likely a Hainaulter born, and so, like Froissart, a native French speaker. Gower wrote copiously in French. Latin was still used as a living tongue, and Gower is again the obvious example with his vast poem, *Vox Clamantis*. The Latin poem of Richard Maidstone, Gaunt's confessor, has been referred to. Maidstone was yet another Merton man. He also composed sermons in Latin, and wrote in English a translation of the Seven Penitential Psalms. He cannot have been unique. Richard Lavenham, another Oxford man, who was Richard's confessor, is not known to have written poetry, but he was a copious writer in Latin and, like Chaucer himself, wrote in English a treatise on the Seven Deadly Sins. Among others might be mentioned Thomas Usk, who wrote the Chaucerian *Testament of Love*; Chaucer's disciple Clanvowe; Hoccleve, a clerk of the Privy Seal, and younger contemporary of Chaucer, who has left some amusing autobiographical poetry about his mildly dissolute life; Lydgate, another younger contemporary, who from the fastness of his monastery poured forth a vast quantity of writing in the early fifteenth century. Some of the alliterative poets, like the author of *Winner and Waster*, certainly knew court life, for that poem centres on Edward III. The second half of the century was a period of great liveliness, with many new forms of writing competing with the old.

Yet there is little to tell us about the place of literature in court life. What little we know is told us by the poets themselves, in incidental remarks of great charm and interest, but neither so full, so realistic, nor probably so unbiased, as we should like for the purpose of social history. Gower tells us at the beginning of the earlier version of his English poem, *Confessio Amantis*, that it is a book written for King Richard's sake, to whom he owes all his

Philippe de Mézières presents his book to King Richard.
See Note on the Wilton Diptych

allegiance. He says he was on a rowing boat on the Thames by London, and

My liege lord par chaunce I mette;	*by*
And so befel, as I cam nyh,	*near*
Out of my bot, whan he me syh,	*boat; saw*
He bad me com in to his barge.	
And whan I was with him at large,	
Amonges othre thinges said,	
He hath this charge upon me leid,	
And bad me doo my besynesse	
That to his hihe worthinesse	
Som newe thing I scholde boke	*make a book of*
That he himself it mihte loke	
After the forme of my writinge.	

This was probably written about 1390, although the time taken to compose so long a work may throw the date of the meeting back some years. Anyway, this looks like a claim for Richard's personal patronage, though the poem also contains a dedication to Henry, son of John of Gaunt. Two or three years later Gower cut out the

reference to Richard, presumably because of his growing unpopularity, and wrote another version of his prologue, saying he had
written the poem 'for England's sake'.

Froissart, towards the end of his great chronicle, tells us how he
longed to see the English court again, having the happiest memories
of his stay there in the time of Edward III and Queen Philippa. He
had some trouble catching up with the court, which was continually
on the move, but eventually, with the help of his old friend, Sir
Richard Stury, he had audience of the King, who was interested in
the book of poems that Froissart wished to present to him. Froissart
says:

> I presented it to him in his chamber, for I had it with me, and laid
> it on his bed. He opened and looked into it with much pleasure. He
> ought to have been pleased, for it was handsomely written and illumin-
> ated, and bound in crimson velvet, with ten silver-gilt studs, and roses
> of the same in the middle, with two large clasps of silver-gilt, richly
> worked with roses in the centre. The King asked me what the book
> treated of: I replied—'Of love!' He was pleased with the answer, and
> dipped into several places, reading parts aloud, for he read and spoke
> French perfectly well, and then gave it to one of his knights, called Sir
> Richard Credon, to carry to his oratory, and made me many acknow-
> ledgements for it.

Froissart also tells us how he read his long romance, *Meliador*, to
another of his patrons, the French Count Gaston de la Foix. Every
night, for some six weeks, after supper, at about midnight, he read
an instalment to the Count and his courtiers. This makes about five
hundred lines a time, and a reading period of about half an hour.
Much courtly literature must have been read in such a way, though
we have no such precise information for the English court. Gower's
enormous *Confessio Amantis*, which consists essentially of a great
number of short stories, would have been very suitable for such
reading.

Portrait of Chaucer commissioned by Hoccleve

Chaucer as usual seems in some way to be in a class of his own. At the beginning of the *Troilus*, where the poet himself is to be imagined to be speaking, he says that he is going to tell the story to his audience 'ere I part from you'. The *Troilus* is over 8,000 lines long, and this, if strictly true, would mean a session of some six hours. In days when people, as in Elizabethan times, could listen to sermons of immense length, this is not impossible. Even today the Russians can listen to speeches six hours long, and the Japanese have a similar heroic capacity even for academic lectures. The well-known manuscript of the *Troilus* in Corpus Christi College, Cambridge, written and illuminated about 1400, shows Chaucer reading to an assembled company of courtiers from a wooden pulpit. It is not a realistic picture; for example, Chaucer is shown without a book before him, and one would have thought that even his astonishing memory would hardly have been capable of exact repetition of so long a poem from memory. And whatever the significance of the background scenes, they are clearly very different from the foreground. But no doubt the picture indicates the sort of circumstance in which courtly poetry might be delivered. In the Household Ordinances of Edward IV, of the fifteenth century, but based on earlier customs, it is said that the esquires of the court (of whom Chaucer was one)

> be accustomed, winter and summer, in afternoons and evenings, to draw to lords' chambers within Court, there to keep honest company after their cunning, in talking of chronicles of kings and of others' policies, or in piping or harping, singings, or other acts martial, to help to occupy the Court, and accompany strangers, till the time require of departing.

This, the only non-literary record, suggests something of the entertainments of music and literature. It suggests the deliberate arrangement of some sort of artistic activity, and shows the typical courtly way of turning entertainment to practical usefulness, and of adorning utility with ceremony and entertainment.

It is also clear that Chaucer at least sometimes wrote to order. This was hardly the case with such a poem as the *Troilus*, but it is obvious that such a poem as *The Book of the Duchess* could not have been written without at least the consent of the bereaved John of Gaunt. And the delightful *Prologue to the Legend of Good Women* represents Chaucer being reproached by 'Alceste' (some great court lady?) for the slander of women in the story of *Troilus*, and ordered to write a series of stories of ladies true in love. But Chaucer didn't finish the series, and if there was ever a public performance it must have been of separate stories.

Another glimpse of literary conditions comes in the long description of Criseyde's meeting with Pandarus in the first part of Book II of the *Troilus*, which is wholly Chaucer's invention. Pandarus discovers Criseyde reading in her paved parlour with her three women; or rather, one of them is reading, and the others are listening. The book is the Romance of Thebes, presumably the twelfth-century Anglo-French version, since women rarely knew Latin. This kind of private reading, where one person reads the book aloud to a group of others, was probably the most usual kind, though private and solitary reading was on the increase. (Pandarus read a romance to himself on the night when Troilus and Criseyde consummated their love.) Group reading is the most useful way of imagining the delivery of poetry in Chaucer's day, because even if private reading was becoming quite common, the style of writing arose directly out of the conditions of group-reading. Henry of Lancaster refers both to those who will *see* his book (i.e. the solitary reader) and those who will *hear* it (the group). The *General Prologue* to *The Canterbury Tales* unquestionably contains a good deal of satire of known individuals, even if we cannot be certain of exactly which individuals, and it is easy to imagine how reading of such writing aloud would have appealed to a group of friends, or a court faction, who relished the unkind portrayal of those in other court factions. At the same time, Chaucer's satire was personal rather than political, and never aimed at anybody really important. His group was perhaps that of the King's chamber knights, including the Lollard knights and others, with important and close relationships with the Lancastrian faction of John of Gaunt and his son Henry, and relations also with the King's mother, Joan of Kent, and those who revered the memory of her husband, the Black Prince.

One must not, in recognising the importance of the familiar group as audience, make too much of division between various court factions. The factions and alliances within the court were much more fluid than we sometimes think. Furthermore, the whole court, friend and foe alike, was frequently meeting together. The different factions were not like the different political parties of a modern Parliament, but much more like the loose groupings and factions that exist within one great political party. Just as such a faction may now have its own recognised spokesmen, its own hard core of supporters, even its own journal, but has also a number of sympathisers, who will not always go all the way with it, so in the fourteenth century there was obviously a number of courtiers, of whom Chaucer was one, with strong sympathies and connections with one or two factions, but never cut off from others, and often on good terms with them. Only in such an atmosphere could poetry like Chaucer's flourish.

Chaucer had too subtle and complex a mind ever to see matters with the simplicity of a politician making an election speech. Nor, as I have shown, had he much interest in those common pursuits dear to the hearts of most Englishmen at all times, which may be summed up as sport—in that time, the tournament, hunting, hawking, and, perhaps we might add, party politics. But even for these very reasons, since he was capable of so wide a range of amused sympathy, since he was orthodox rather than rebellious, wise as well as cynical, he makes an extraordinarily good spokesman for the court-culture of Richard's reign, and for chivalry as it was then understood. Furthermore, we can actually read what he himself has to say. And since he wrote fiction, and was a great poet, he speaks without arguing for himself, and with great richness of meaning and implication. The whole body of his work, but above all *The Knight's Tale*, is the great document of courtly and knightly values in this period. In *The Knight's Tale* we find the court as the centre of the kingdom, with its concerns for war and justice, but also its leisure, its delight in hunting and tournament. The younger people are chiefly concerned with love and war, but Theseus, the wise king, and his father, can make a sober assessment of the whole of life. Religion, philosophy and science find a place in controlling and interpreting the harsh chances of life. For all the splendours of the court, the raptures of love, and the glories of martial success, much, perhaps most of life, is hard, and there is plenty of suffering. It is a sympathetic poem, but there is also a note of stern resignation, and a resolute will 'to make a virtue of necessity' as Theseus says. And there is also a note of flippant hardness which is one of Chaucer's most constant features, and which is very difficult to describe in modern terms, because it lies alongside, yet does not, as one might have thought, cancel out, the positive ideals, values and sympathies. Even when we have made allowance for Chaucer's remarkable genius, we must also agree that the court and the chivalric code which could help to produce this blend of love and loyalty and gaiety, bravery and pity, *franchise*, generosity, and courtesy, philosophical and worldly wit and wisdom, was one of the greatest achievements in the history of English civilisation.

A NOTE ON THE WILTON DIPTYCH

This very beautiful example of late-fourteenth century court art has been claimed for both French and English. Mr Harvey, in his *Gothic England*, London, 1948, analyses the style of the picture and suggests that it was painted by an Englishman, possibly Thomas Litlynton.

The subject of the picture is the presentation of Richard II by St John the Baptist (on the eve of whose feast Richard was crowned) and by the English Royal saints, Edmund the Martyr (with the arrow) and Edward the Confessor (both from the Anglo-Saxon period), to the Virgin and Child with angels.

Some have thought this to be a coronation picture, but it has some puzzling features. According to Miss M. V. Clarke, *Fourteenth Century Studies*, Oxford, 1937, the badge of the White Hart, which was Richard's personal badge and is everywhere in the picture, was introduced late in the reign. Again, there appears on the back of one of the panels of the diptych a shield bearing the arms of Edward the Confessor. There was a cult of the Confessor at Richard's court as part of the cult of royalty, but it was not till 1395 that Richard took the Confessor's arms as part of his own. In the picture Richard's collar of broom-cods is very noticeable. Miss Clarke considered that it was meant to represent one given to Richard by the French King Charles VI about 1396. It would seem, then, that the picture comes from near the end of Richard's reign, 1396-9. But then why should he be represented so young? Other pictures show him with a double beard, and in later years a decidedly cunning expression. The answer may be that he is here deliberately flattered and idealised with an appearance of youth and hope. The banner may be compared with the banner in an illumination in a manuscript which shows a book being presented to Richard (see illustration p. 196). The book so presented to Richard, and which carries the illumination of its own presentation and the banner, is an address to Richard in French encouraging him to undertake a crusade. The author of this book, Philippe de Mézières, spent a lifetime trying to encourage European sovereigns and nobles to undertake a new crusade. The splendid *entremés* put on in Paris in 1378 (see p. 182) was one of his more elaborate pieces of propaganda. He also presented to the Earl of Huntingdon an illuminated manuscript which has some details that recall the Wilton Diptych. The books presented to Richard and the Earl, and the banner which also appears in the Wilton Diptych, are all to do with the crusading Order of the Passion which Philippe wished to found. The significance of the Wilton Diptych, then, would seem to be that it urges an idealised and therefore flattered Richard, the descendant and inheritor of the saintly kings of England, to undertake a crusade. The collar of broom-cods, which was the badge of the French King, shows that the crusade should be undertaken together with the French.

If this explanation is correct the picture is an interesting example of how court art and ceremonial could be used to serve practical religious and political ends. It remains a very beautiful picture!

CHAPTER SEVEN

Courtesy comes from Heaven

IN an earlier chapter I quoted the line from a courtesy book that 'courtesy comes from heaven'. *The Knight's Tale* shows at a deeper level some of the ways in which chivalric courtesy was penetrated by religious feeling and thought, even if flavoured by a dash of cynicism. Not everyone was so deeply affected, but the influence of religion, even in the courtly life, was strong both at superficial and deeper levels. All levels of society took shape from religion, and God seemed very near in the fourteenth century, sometimes. During the synod at Blackfriars which was examining Wycliffe's heresies in 1382, an earthquake occurred. This was taken both by the Wycliffites and the anti-Wycliffites as a sign of God's deep and immediate concern with the question in hand, though as may be imagined each side interpreted His anger very differently. Religion was for many reasons a dominating force in most people's lives. Birth, education, marriage, death, were marked by religious seriousness and ceremony, invested with all the significance of eternity. There was no rival to the Church's organisation both in the realms of thought and in earthly forms. Almost all intellectual life was carried on by clerics. The biggest building most people entered was a church. Apart from armies, the largest gatherings were for religious occasions. The pageantry of kings was sanctified by religion. The calendar was regulated by the liturgy as much as by the needs of the seasons. Deeds of good nature and charity were encouraged by the Church, in whose keeping were the moral laws essential to the survival of any community. Violence, lust, selfishness, fraud and deceit, in practical affairs as well as in the spiritual life, were constantly condemned by preachers. A holiday was a holy day. Such entertainment as the drama, popular throughout the country as drama never has been since, arose from the services of the Church, and was based on the Bible.

The upper classes, as usual in England from Augustine's conversion of King Ethelbert of Kent in 596, were more convinced Christians than the lower. What pagan survivals there were, such as May-festivals and folk-plays, were pretty well restricted to the poor and ignorant, except when they were, as in the Maying, somewhat delicately imitated. In the court, and among the upper classes, even among merchants, it was common to attend Mass in the early part of the day, as happens in Chaucer's *Shipman's Tale*. Everywhere we see the observance of religious forms. When Richard ordered the arrest of his uncle the Earl of Gloucester, Gloucester was captured while taking part in a religious procession at the collegiate church which he had recently founded.

Yet Gloucester was less of a saint than most. And he *was* arrested, by Richard himself, in the midst of religious duties, and his death in prison was probably connived at by Richard. Moreover, when Richard himself was eventually captured at Flint Castle at the end of his reign, he was betrayed by the breaking of a safe-conduct which had been sworn by the most sacred oath, that on the consecrated Host at the altar. If God was very near, and the thought and forms of religion were everywhere, both could be flouted outrageously. It seems that if the upper classes were the most Christian, they were also the worst sinners. But at all levels corruption and abuse, as every reader of Chaucer's *Prologue* knows, flourished alongside beautiful and necessary ideals.

One of the reasons was the extreme emphasis placed on the 'last things'; on death and on Heaven, Hell, and Purgatory, to all of which the Church held the gate—not for nothing had the Pope assumed the power of St Peter's keys. So life might be lived wickedly, in the hope of having time to repent just before the end. This made for a mixture of spiritual power and ineffectualness of the Church which is well illustrated by a personal anecdote by Bishop Brinton, or Brunton.

> At the time I was studying at Cambridge [he says] there was a certain boatman called Roger, who was excommunicated by name by the chancellor of the university, because of his crimes and open acts of contempt. He took no notice of the sentence and went to Lynn for a little while. Then, when he had been drinking a lot with some of his friends for a long time, he began to stare at the wall and shout out horribly, 'Alas, alas, I have been excommunicated.' When he was asked by his companions what was the reason for such a sudden sorrow, he told them he had been excommunicated by the chancellor of Cambridge, and despaired of the salvation of his soul. They advised him to go back with them to Cambridge, that he might humbly seek and obtain his safety and absolution from the said chancellor. He agreed, and went on to a boat with them. When they came near the Magdalen bridge at Wiggenhall he suddenly broke away from them, and wished to drown himself; but he was held by his companions and tied up for a time. When he saw that he could not escape from their hands by his own strength, he pretended that he wanted to help them at the oars, so that they might go more quickly, which they allowed him to do. And so, by the prompting of the devil, by Priest's House, he jumped into the water. They turned the boat back, and held out the oars, but he despised their help, and howled, 'Alas that I was ever born, because I am damned by excommunication.' And so in despair he was miserably drowned. Less than three days after I was returning from the schools to Lynn, and when I heard of the case I was sorry, because he used to bring letters to me from my friends. I asked to see his body, and though in life he had been tall and handsome, in death I saw him black and deformed.

The embodiment of orthodox religious feeling among the upper classes was the Black Prince, who towards the end of his life was taken to be the leader, or at least the supporter, of clerical interests in the court, while his brother Gaunt (who was personally no less, nor more, devout than his elder brother) was a leader of an anti-clerical party. When the Black Prince brought his captive, King John of France, home to England, he stopped for a day, according to Froissart, at Canterbury cathedral, where both he and John made offerings. In 1363 he founded at Canterbury a chantry chapel, whose remains are still to be seen in the crypt, in which two priests were to pray for his soul during his life and after his death. Such a foundation was becoming increasingly common, and when a man could not afford to found one for himself, he often joined a gild which provided a chantry and priest for the members jointly. To pay for his chantry the Prince gave an estate to the Cathedral which it still possessed in the nineteenth century. When the Prince lay dying in 1376 he made a will by which he ordered his burial in Canterbury. This he signed on 7th June. On the 8th he sank rapidly. The poem by Chandos Herald describes his end. He caused his rooms to be opened, and all his followers to come in. He asked pardon of all those who had so faithfully served him, whom he could not sufficiently reward. God and His saints would repay them, he said, and they all wept and mourned. He recommended to them his little son, Richard, and asked them to serve him as faithfully as they had served himself. Then he called the King, and his brother Gaunt, and commended his son and wife to them. They both swore upon the Bible to look after them—a promise that was kept. The Prince for some time felt such great pain that he cried out, to the great grief of all that were watching him. His men, down to the youngest page, were constantly passing and re-passing to see their dying master, and one rather strange incident occurred. Sir Richard Stury came in, the old acquaintance of Froissart and Chaucer, later a faithful knight of Richard's and of the Prince's widow, Joan of Kent, friend of Clifford and Latimer, and like them attracted to Lollardy. When the Prince saw him he immediately reproached him angrily, told him to leave the room and see him no more. This spurt of his old proud irritable spirit exhausted the Prince who fell back in a faint. When he recovered, the Bishop of Bangor, who was attending his deathbed, urged him to forgive all his enemies and to ask forgiveness of God and men. The Prince replied, 'I will.' The Bishop was not satisfied, and urged him again, to say it in so many words. But the Prince would only repeat, 'I will.' The Bishop said, 'An evil spirit holds his tongue—we must drive it away, or he will die in his sins.' He sprinkled the room with holy water and the Prince gave way. He joined his hands in prayer and gave thanks to God for all his benefits, and prayed for forgiveness from God and from all men whom he had offended. With these words 'the flower of English knighthood' as Froissart calls him, died in the palace of Westminster, at 3 p.m. on Trinity Sunday, a festival he had always had in special reverence. He had deeply caught the English imagination, and perhaps no prince or king up to his time had been so deeply mourned.

How starkly, though not unemotionally, death was faced! No concealment from the sufferer, no drugged sleep but a deep anxiety to bring about repentance and reconcilement. It is in the tradition of great deaths, as striking, if not so greatly moving, as the death of a greater hero, Lord Nelson. Twentieth-century medicine and the change or failure of religious beliefs have now made such scenes impossible, but they are not to be condemned as morbid.

The Prince's will, in French, begins formally:

In the name of the Father, the Son, and the Holy Spirit, Amen. We, Edward, eldest son of the King of England and of France, Prince of Wales, Duke of Cornwall, and Count of Chester, the seventh day of June, the year of grace 1376, in our chamber within the palace of our most redoutable lord and father the King at Westminster, being of good and sound memory, and in consideration of the short extent of human frailty, and how uncertain is the time of its dissolution according to the divine will, and constantly wishing to be ready to the help of God in its disposition, we ordain and make our testament in the manner following. First, we bequeathe our soul to God our Creator, and to the holy blessed Trinity, and to the glorious Virgin Mary, and to all the saints; and our body to be buried in the Cathedral Church of the Trinity at Canterbury.

He gives elaborate instructions as to how and where he is to be buried, which suggest he was far from forgetting worldly glory. By contrast, Clifford, who was a Lollard for a long time, describes himself in his will as 'God's traitor', refers to his 'wretched and sinful soul', and asks that his 'wretched carrion' be buried in the farthest corner of the churchyard. Whether or not this shows repentance for Lollardy, it well illustrates the different temper that was attracted to Lollardy, and recalls the terms of several other Lollard or ex-Lollard wills.

The Black Prince's will goes on to quote the French verses, well-known at the time, which he wished to have on his tomb. With their emphasis on corruption, their grim reminder that riches, power, and beauty are temporary and must be given up, they are typical of one rather unspiritual aspect of religion at the time. I give a rough translation:

> You who pass with pursed-up mouth,
>   Where this body lies,
> Hear what I must say to you,
>   As I can devise.
> Such as you are, so once was I;
>   You will be like me:
> To death I never gave a thought,
>   I lived delightfully.
> On earth I had such riches great,
>   They made a noble show—
> Land and mansions, clothes and gold,
>   Horses, here below.

But now I am poor and despised,
    Beneath the earth I lie;
My lovely form is all away,
    In flesh I putrefy.
A narrow house I live in now;
    The truth only is here.
And surely if you saw my face,
    It hardly would appear
That I was once like you a man,
    For death has changed me whole.
In mercy pray to Heaven's King
    That he may save my soul.
All those who now will for me pray,
    With God to make my peace,
May God set them in Paradise,
    Where joy can never cease.

The will bequeathes in detail the Prince's earthly personal posses-sions. Among his religious possessions were a missal and a breviary, books which he says 'we have had made and illuminated with our arms in various places, and also with our badges of ostrich feathers'. These splendid service books were to remain for ever in the use of the Cathedral. He also bequeathed 'our great table of silver and gold, full of precious relics, and in the middle a cross made from the wood of the Holy Cross, and the said table is decorated with precious stones and pearls, namely, twenty-five rubies, thirty-four sapphires, fifty-eight big pearls, and several other sapphires, emeralds and little pearls, to the high altar of our (religious) house of Ashridge, which is of our foundation'. It is no wonder, when one considers such gifts from rich men, many of which went to Canterbury, that when the shrine of Becket was looted at the Reformation, men carried away twenty-four cartloads of the richest treasure. And these gifts also give some idea of the incredible treasures that adorned the altars and shrines of the great churches of the land, giving glamour, beauty and superstition to the practice of religion, arousing wonder, awe, devotion, and greed.

The embalmed and coffined body of the Black Prince lay in state at Westminster for no less than four months, and then was taken to Canterbury. The hearse was drawn by twelve black horses, and the whole court, and both Houses of Parliament, followed in deep mourning. Presumably Chaucer was there too. The Prince had instructed that two war-horses with trappings of his arms and badges, and two men dressed in his livery and wearing his helmets, should walk in front of the corpse. From Westminster it went towards London, and then along the same way that Chaucer's pilgrims and many thousands of others before and since followed to the great shrine at Canterbury. It passed through the fields of the little village

Lydgate and the Canterbury Pilgrims leaving Canterbury

of Charing, by St Martin's and Queen Eleanor's cross, at Charing, along the Strand, past the great houses of the nobles, and Gaunt's palace of the Savoy, soon to be burnt down, where the Prince's prisoner King John had once been lodged. Then by St Paul's and down the steep hill to the river and over London Bridge, the only way of crossing the Thames, and so through Southwark, by the Tabard Inn, where Chaucer was to describe the meeting of his pilgrims. The distance from Southwark to Canterbury along the Dover Road, or Pilgrims' Way, the usual route, which the Prince's body would have taken, is about fifty-six miles. A hard-riding messenger of the King's household might do it in a day, or just over. Pilgrims might take two or three days, and a funeral procession, as it wound over rutted roads through the autumn countryside, might take more. When the procession, which, if it did not include all who had started out must still have been large and impressive, reached the west gate of Canterbury, it was met, if the instructions in the will were obeyed (not all of them were), by two armed knights on horseback, one bearing the Prince's warlike motto, *Houmout*—'High Courage'— and his arms of England and France, the other armed in black, with the ostrich feathers, and perhaps his motto of peace '*Ich dien*'—'I serve'. Four black banners followed. The body was placed in the cathedral between the High Altar and the choir, surrounded with burning candles. Black hangings trimmed with crimson and richly embroidered were hung around, while the funeral services were read in the presence of the great men of the land. The Prince had directed that he should lie near his chapel in the crypt, but he was finally entombed where he still lies, in a space now crowded, but then nearly empty, and dominated by the splendour of Becket's shrine. Tomb and shrine have lost their riches and gilded brightness now, but there they remain today, with the Prince's great helmet, his gauntlet, and other possessions still to be seen above his effigy in full armour, his hands joined in prayer, his face with its flat Plantagenet cheeks, bold nose, and severe expression, his head resting on his helmet. The verses quoted in his will, slightly altered, are carved about his tomb. The sense of glory and of sin, the recognition of corruption, the hope of Heaven, all characteristic of the courtly and usual religion of the times, here reach their full expression.

There had been a church in Canterbury in Roman times. When Augustine baptised Ethelbert of Kent in 596, Ethelbert granted to Augustine some land, and his own palace, which then became the first cathedral church in Canterbury. Of this nothing now remains, and the present great church was begun in the eleventh century. For centuries, however, the cathedral had been overshadowed in fame by the neighbouring Abbey of St Augustine. The event which gave the cathedral its European fame, and led people in the later medieval centuries to regard it as the most sacred spot in England, was the murder of Becket in 1170. In the fourteenth century all classes made it an object of pilgrimage, and many people came from foreign countries, while pilgrimages themselves, as *The Canterbury Tales* shows, became a blend of devotional exercise and popular holiday. It became the custom for the bands of pilgrims to be accompanied by hired minstrels and story-tellers, so that while Chaucer's scheme in his great work is in itself obviously unrealistic, it is all the same grounded in fact. The orthodox who defended pilgrimages thought it not unreasonable that people should be cheered on their way by such devices. The enemies of pilgrimages, such as the Lollards, asserted that the minstrels were hired to sing wanton songs, 'and then, if these men and women be half a month out of their pilgrimage, many of them shall be half a year after great jugglers, story-tellers, and liars'. A 'Canterbury Tale' came to mean a 'lying story'. Even the orthodox commented on the abuses of pilgrimage. Archbishop Sudbury himself, when Bishop of London, once told a crowd of pilgrims that it was vain to hope for good from the indulgence of penance which they expected to gain from the pilgrimage. They cursed him for his pains, and prayed he might meet a shameful death. Since he was also tolerant of Lollardy, not a few Londoners thought he had no more than his deserts when in the Revolt the peasants beheaded him. Here as elsewhere we see the difficulties that the medieval church had in controlling and disciplining people in line with its sometimes impractical ideals; the old Adam was strong. And as usual the Lollards appear as taking to an extreme what many serious-minded orthodox folk already thought, developing the criticism that already existed, rather than making a completely new departure.

The inside of the cathedral was a crowded and brilliant sight, which to the eyes of most modern Englishmen would undoubtedly now seem distressingly tawdry. The walls and ceilings were brightly painted, cloth hangings being fixed to rods which may still be seen running along from pillar to pillar. There was no clear view along the body of the church as now; it was full of chapels, altars, and chantries, with their images painted in lifelike colours and all with precious adornments. The stained glass was some of the best in Europe, and filled not only the choir windows, as now, but also the windows of the nave. In the Reformation 'Blue Dick' of Canterbury took a ladder and a lance and found great satisfaction in the nave in 'rattling down old Becket's glassy bones', though some of what he destroyed was put there during the fifteenth century.

There was no pious hush in the cathedral. There were usually many visitors, not always well behaved. The anonymous poet of *The Tale of Beryn* in the early part of the fifteenth century takes Chaucer's own pilgrims into the church. The Knight puts the pilgrims in their proper order, and a monk sprinkles them with holy water. The respectable characters behave respectably, but the Friar makes an attempt to see the nun's face more closely, and those 'lewd sots' the Pardoner and the Miller fall into a heated argument about the meanings of the pictures in the stained glass, which they cannot understand. They are reproached by the Host, and at last even they are awed into quietness and decency before the wonders of the relics and the shrine.

The relics of Thomas Becket himself were shown; there was part of his skull, encased in silver, which was presented to be kissed, and his shirt and drawers of hair-cloth—the painful clothes of secret penance which had so impressed his monks when they discovered them after his death. There was also a great mass of more ordinary relics, many to be kissed, including the arm of St George himself, now for some time accepted as the patron saint of England. Ordinary people were not permitted to see the most precious of these relics. But everyone was shown the statue of the Virgin, covered with pearls and precious stones, which foreign pilgrims were told had often spoken to Thomas when he prayed to it.

The shrine was set behind the High Altar. Dean Stanley, whose account in *Historical Memorials of Canterbury*[1] has been mainly followed here, says that what seems to have impressed every pilgrim as absolutely peculiar to Canterbury was the long succession of ascents, by which 'church seemed to be piled on church'. Up these long steps the pilgrims mounted, or probably crawled on their knees, and the way the steps are worn shows what numbers there once were. Nothing at all now remains of the shrine. It must have been one of the most astonishing sights of Europe, apart from its religious significance. The lower part of the shrine was stone, supported by arches, and sick and lame pilgrims were allowed to place themselves between these, rubbing their afflicted limbs against the marble which held the body. The shrine proper was at first invisible, concealed by a wooden canopy; at a sign this was raised, and the shrine appeared blazing with gold and innumerable jewels. While the pilgrims knelt, an officer of the monastery came forward and pointed out the various jewels with a white wand, naming them

[1] Dean Stanley, *Historical Memorials of Canterbury*, John Murray, 1854.

After visiting a shrine the pilgrim would buy a badge, as a souvenir or as a talisman.
This badge shows St Thomas of Canterbury

in English and, for the benefit of foreigners, in French, telling their
values and the marvellous magical properties which were normally
attributed to jewels in the Middle Ages. The figure of an angel
pointed to the greatest of them, a ruby or diamond, said by some to
be as large as a hen's egg, by others as a thumb-nail, given to the
shrine by Louis VII of France when he came on pilgrimage, and to

216

which various legends were attached. Then the canopy descended and the pilgrims turned away, saying their prayers, and dropping their offerings into the boxes which stood ready at the foot of the stairs. The possession of the relics of a popular saint was a most important item in the finances of a church or monastery.

One of the last things a pilgrim would do when he left the place of pilgrimage would be to acquire a pilgrim sign. All shrines sold such things; the sign for Canterbury was a brooch of lead or silver, representing either a little jar, or the mitred head of St Thomas. They were bought, along with a number of other souvenirs, jars of water with magic powers to cure, and such like, from the shops and stalls in Mercery Street, which was then arcaded, like the famous 'Rows' of Chester and many an Italian town still. Indeed, something of the atmosphere of medieval Canterbury is still to be caught at famous shrines of the present day, in France and Italy, India and Japan.

After the visit to the shrine the pilgrims employed themselves like any tourists, some respectably and some not. There were many inns in the town and here they stayed, perhaps only for the night, before going back to London. No one can make a profit-and-loss account for such activities as pilgrimages. For those who were seriously and piously inclined they had an obvious value. For most people they had at least the virtue of making holy lives more easily imaginable and remembered, just as a visit to a museum makes the past more real by the actual sight of objects descended from the past. They provided an excellent holiday, and that is always a good thing. Yet they also provided unlimited opportunity for abuse. Many of the practices they encouraged were recognised by finer minds as rank superstition. If we may judge that those who behaved badly on pilgrimage would have done so anyway, yet the pilgrimage gave a special opportunity for bad behaviour that was singularly out of tune with its proper purpose.

The Norwich Retable,

Such events as the Black Prince's death, and such 'institutions' as the pilgrimage to Canterbury, give something of the note of popular religion among all classes, courtly and other. The force of religion gave rise to thousands of acts of charity and holiness which otherwise would have been lacking—witness the hundreds of hospitals for the poor and sick in London alone—but one is also struck by the misunderstandings, to call them no more, and the abuses. There was not much downright atheism. Very rarely does one come across an individual who is thought to have been an atheist. There was a good deal of scepticism of various kinds, chiefly arising out of the course of philosophical thought at Oxford. Lollardy, with its contempt for images, is another kind of scepticism. There was certainly a vein of humorous scepticism in Chaucer himself, and there are other traces of it in court circles. But this seems

late fourteenth century

never to have seriously worked against religious belief, especially when men came near the end of their lives. The real opposition to religion as such came from the nature of men themselves, from their will, corrupted, as the age saw it, by Adam's fall. The slightest knowledge of the *General Prologue* to *The Canterbury Tales*, to go no farther, shows how often even clerics fell below the ideal. There were worse abuses, like the scandalous 'crusade' organised by Despenser, the fighting Bishop of Norwich, against the Flemish who adhered to the other Pope, not supported by the English, at the time of the Great Schism, when there were two Popes, each fighting the other. The Schism itself is of course an example of the failure of Christendom on a European scale, while Norwich's crusade was merely an opportunity for looting and pillage, though many English people supported it with almost hysterical fervour.

When men are so violent, it is clear that continual force of persuasion and threats is necessary to restrain them. The wonder is, not that the Church so often failed, but that it so often succeeded in imposing a sense of orderliness and decency, of worship and spirituality, on an unruly society. The ideal of an orderly, decent, church-attending life was not then so unspiritual as it may sometimes now be presented. Nor was continual exhortation so banal when it was met with such outbreaks of violence and abuse as were common in the age.

The general ideal of the Christian life for all classes is well described by Langland, who writes much better than most of the preachers.

> For Holy Church commands all manner of people
> Under obedience to be, and obedient to the law.
> First, religious men [i.e. monks] of religion their rule to hold,
> And under obedience to be, by days and nights;
> Lewd [i.e. ignorant] men to labour; and lords to hunt
> In woods and forests, for fox and other beasts
> That in wild woods be, and in waste places,
> As wolves that worry men, women and children;
> And upon Sundays to cease, God's service to hear,
> Both Matins and Mass, and after meat, in churches
> To hear Evensong every man ought.
> Thus it behoves for lord, for learned, and lewd,
> Each holyday to hear wholly the service;
> Vigils and fasting days, furthermore, to know,
> And fulfil these fastings (except for infirmity),
> Poverty and other penances, like pilgrimages and toiling.
> Under this obedience are we each one.
> Whoso breaks this, be well aware, unless he repent,
> Amend himself, and mercy ask, and meekly confess,
> I dread me, if he die, it would as deadly sin
> Be accounted before Christ, unless Conscience excuse him.

Piers Plowman, CX, ll. 219 ff.

At a higher social level we have an example in the sermons of Bishop Brinton, who was not so much of a national civil servant as some bishops were, and who, of a modest and holy life, often addressed the court in sermons, of which the notes in Latin have recently been edited for the Camden Society by Sister Mary Devlin. He is a type of the ideal sincere churchman, confident of his own position and the truth he holds, and unlike many others never afraid to speak out. 'We prelates, having the cure of souls and being preachers,' he says in one sermon, 'who are the light of the world and salt of the earth, let us not put up with errors in the people but rather let us destroy them and preach solid truths.' He was not afraid to criticise anyone, either clergy or lay, high or low. He attacks the friars for hearing confessions. On the other hand, he is never tired of telling his own clergy their faults. He was prominent also in the arguments against Wycliffe, who would have impoverished and disestablished the Church. He condemned the Peasants' Revolt:

> Any sudden insurrection is abominable and worthy of condemnation for two reasons: first because since servitude was introduced into the world by sin, justice demands that masters should rule over their servants, and that servants should be subject to their masters. . . . Secondly servants who have been made masters do not know how to govern.[1]

It is good sound conservative stuff, voicing the normal opinion of those responsible for government, and of men like Chaucer, Langland, and Gower, even though Brinton was himself apparently of low birth, and has the age's sympathy for the poor. Nor does he hold back from criticising the knightly class. In the funeral sermon he gave for the Black Prince, whom he much admired, when he has praised his virtues, and held up the ideal of knighthood, insisting that it should be pure especially from bodily stain, he goes on:

[1] Transl. by Sister Mary Devlin, Vol. I, p. xxxl.

Who then can be surprised if the English are unfortunate in war when on all sides there reign lust, adultery, incest, because few people, and especially lords, are contented with their wives . . . [and] we prelates for the most part for love, or fear, or favour, fall away from justice, because we cite, suspend, and excommunicate people of little importance, and the poor, who have only moderately sinned. But in correcting lords and powerful people, however notoriously great criminals they are, we are silent. . . .

But towards the end of his active life he had to say:

I say for my part with tears that for these past ten years I have preached against the sins prevalent in my diocese, nor, however, have I seen anyone rise effectually from sin. . . . For what adulterer having given up his mistress is faithful to his lawful wife? What usurer restores what he has unjustly taken? What unjust maintainer [i.e. a lord who kept a private army] or false witness refrains from his sins? What user of fraudulent weights and measures through which he has deceived his neighbours and poor wayfarers has broken or burned them? [1]

Brinton stands for the thousands of preachers and moralists and literary satirists who gently or roughly, solemnly, or, like Chaucer, with comic ridicule, advised, sneered, threatened, cursed the faults of the age, and saw little hope or sign of improvement. Yet the power of words, though indirect, is not small. Gradually men's minds are changed. And even in the fourteenth century such constant exhortation had its effects. Most of Brinton's efforts, and those of other preachers, were not devoted to social commentary but to the spiritual teachings of Christianity, which certainly had, or ought to have had, moral and social implications, but whose centre was not in morality or society. The centre of the religious acts of the day was the priest's turning bread and wine into the body of God; the offices of the Church were centred on worship, not to be measured by other yardsticks than the spiritual—which is not a yardstick. Yet we can find evidences of the workings of the spiritual

[1] Sister Mary Devlin's translation, p. xxiv.

ideal in a positive way, in literature especially, and not least in courtly literature. Chaucer's noble description of the Parson is one; but the example which is nearest to a straightforward document is the book already quoted several times for what it tells us about social life, *Le Livre de Seyntz Medicines* by Henry of Lancaster, edited for the Anglo-Norman Text Society in 1940 by E. J. Arnould. Although Henry was famous in his own day for his soldiership, courtesy, and goodness, an historian would not have guessed the deep spiritual source of his life if this book of his had not been found. Without being morbid he is deeply conscious of his sins, and says that it is a relief to him to think, write and speak about them, though he is careful to do so in a way that does not pander to sensationalism. He has both social and spiritual good taste and his book is most attractive in tone—manly, sincere, honest, devout, and fresh. Its name comes from the holy medicines that Christian faith provides for sin. These 'medicines' are of various kinds: contemplation of Christ's Passion, the five joys of Mary, a proper understanding of our misfortunes in the world; all the physical illness we have is 'a precious medicine for curing us of our great sickness of sin'. His comfort in spite of all his sins and wilful neglect is that since His Ascension Christ 'has comforted us by coming amongst us, and in the form of bread we can see him when and as often as we wish; and if we need it, because of sickness of body or of soul, the good Lord is most ready to enter in us and visit us within and without and deliver us from all infirmities and evils'. Nor, of course, is this the work of one who does not know the pleasures and vices of the world. He makes an elaborate comparison of his heart to a city's market-place where

> most men are drunk, and taverns are situated near and all around the market, so that men eat and drink so much that they can only leave them with great difficulty, they are so drunk, and their bellies so full; and the cooks and the taverners do not stop crying their good food and

the good wine; truly they praise them quite differently from what they are worth, for they cry that they are good, and very often they are extremely bad. And those things signify the evil acquaintances and the dirty words from which evil deeds follow; and silly women dress themselves up on market-day better than they do on Easter Day to catch and hang on to fools; and there are enough and more than enough of such who do not come to the market for any other kind of goods, and even though they have only one penny they will sooner use it in the house and hospital of the Dèvil . . . than they will divide it among the poor in the house of God.

This is something of a commonplace, but freshly and vigorously written, with characteristic energy.

What is most characteristic of Henry of Lancaster is, as we should expect, the generally chivalric cast of his mind. Many of his personal observations on courtly life have been quoted already, but it goes deeper than such surface comments. He tends to see Christ as a courtly superior; Christ is 'a good lord, so brave, so sweet, so very courteous [*debonaire*]'. Sweet, and especially 'debonair' were very popular courtly words, used both for secular and religious writing. The lover in *The Romaunt of the Rose* is described as sweet and debonair; Chaucer uses both words often. Henry several times calls himself a traitor to God, and says that although God has paid so great a ransom for him as the sacrifice of His own Son, he has often voluntarily gone back to the prison of Hell. It is, however, the humility of God which especially strikes Henry, naturally enough. As a great lord himself he knows what humility costs. Humility is especially seen as part of Christ's *courtesy*, the virtue of courts. 'He is a courteous lord and good to serve, and so humble that he very willingly shows himself in a little crumb of bread.' 'Lord, I understand that you are so courteous that you will deny nothing to a person in need who asks from his heart.' This emphasis on courtliness as a high expression of Christianity is an important one in the fourteenth century. Henry of Lancaster and the Black Prince, as well as many bishops and humbler souls, show some of the ways in which it was possible to combine the ideals and desires of secular life with those of the accepted Christian doctrine. The alliterative poets and the Lollard movement show other ways.

The alliterative poet or poets who wrote *Sir Gawain and the Green Knight* and *Pearl* somewhere in the North-west Midlands have often been mentioned. They give evidence of a responsible serious audience, as courtly as Chaucer's audience in the King's court, but more old-fashioned in its patriotism and beliefs. The religious feeling in these poems differs from that of Chaucer's, just as other feelings differ. What is striking about them is the way they combine the idealised courtly ideal with Christian doctrine, not in a rather superficial orthodoxy, like the Black Prince, but with a deep sincerity. *Pearl*, which is probably the greatest of these poems, as it is undoubtedly one of the great poems in the language, praises the Mother of Jesus as 'the queen of courtesy', and the very word 'courtesy' itself is used for the divine Grace. In a way we are reminded of Henry of Lancaster, but the poem develops the attitudes found in him with all the powers of great art, and there is no conflict felt between courtliness and Christianity. In *Sir Gawain and the Green Knight* the presentation of courtliness as the height of Christianity is everywhere. Gawain himself is the perfect knight and the perfect Christian; devout in religious observance, chaste, humble, brave, well dressed, and perfectly mannered. Although the essence of the latter part of the poem is his dilemma between preserving his chastity against the lady's assaults, and preserving the perfect good manners which must never rebuff a lady, it is a dilemma between two ideals which are felt to be part of one greater whole, the ideal of 'the verray parfit gentle knight'. There is no feeling that the courtly ideal of the great warrior Gawain may itself be entirely wrong.

Contrast this courtly Christianity with the following condemnation of the courtly life, written at about the same date.

> For before God, all virtue is honour and all sin is shame. And in this world it is ever the reverse. For the world holds them worshipful that be great warriors and fighters, and that destroy and win many lands, and waste and give much food to them that have enough, and that spend outrageously in meat and drink, in clothing, in building, and in living in ease and sloth and many other sins. And also the world worships them much that will be avenged proudly and despitously of every wrong that is said or done to them. And of such folk men make books and songs, and read and sing of them, for to hold the memory of their deeds the longer here upon earth. For that is a thing that worldly men desire greatly, that their name might last long after them here upon earth ... [such folk as wish to live quietly and sparingly and modestly] the world scorneth, and holds them lollers and rascals, fools, and shameful wretches ... and therefore take we savour in those things that be so worshipful and so good above, and care we never though the world scorn us, or hold us wretches. For the world scorned Christ and held Him a fool; and all that He suffered patiently.

Here is the complete condemnation of lives such as that of the Black Prince, and of the poem by Chandos Herald which celebrates and preserves his name. The glories of blood and state, the high court art, the splendid buildings, the noble ardours of chivalric war, such as we find at the court of Edward or of Richard, are seen as sin and shame. This is much harsher than the condemnations of Henry of Lancaster. It goes farther even than Bishop Brinton in his condemnation of war and self-glorification. It looks like the work of one of those Poor Preachers whom Wycliffe is thought to have inspired, for the author clearly sees himself as one of those whom the world despises as a 'loller'. The word 'loller' originally meant 'idler', but it was often applied at this time sneeringly to those who were more rightly called 'Lollards', after a Dutch word which was the name of a similar religious group in the Low Countries. The author in fact seems to be a Lollard, taking the normal condemnations by the medieval church of worldliness and wickedness a stage further. One might imagine him as a poor cleric rightly incensed at the bad and unchristian behaviour of the courtly classes. The astonishing thing is that the author was a knight of Richard's court, a poetic disciple of Chaucer's, Sir John Clanvowe. This extract, slightly modernised, comes from a treatise, not yet printed, in a manuscript of University College, Oxford, now in the Bodleian Library, which is headed, 'This treatise next following made Sir John Clanvowe knight, the last voyage that he made over the Great Sea in which he died; of whose soul Jesus have mercy.'

Clanvowe's treatise emphasises the strange situation of a number of knights, and of Chaucer himself, at the end of the century, in Richard's court. They were deeply committed to the courtly life, because of its imaginative and emotional attractions, its material rewards, its necessary existence as government. Much of the weight of normal religious teaching emphasised the necessity of government, of having inferiors and superiors, or lords living a life different from others. Many quotations from Langland, Brinton, and others already made in this book have illustrated this normal orthodox view. At the same time the medieval church was equally deeply committed not merely to a belief in the partial and limited importance of worldly experience in the total scheme of things, but in the world's almost complete corruption and worthlessness. As Chaucer puts it into the mouth of Theseus, this life is 'a foul prison'. And as Chaucer expresses it for himself, in a poem to his friend Sir Philip de la Vache, advising him not to be in thrall to 'the world',

Her is non hoom, her nis but wildernesse.   *home; is not*

This attitude of contempt of the world naturally condemned courtliness because it was, even when virtuous, the extreme example of worldly life.

Contempt for the world had flourished in medieval religious theory for many centuries; its supreme expression was monasticism. It was natural enough for clerics to preach it. What made the situation different towards the end of the fourteenth century was that laymen, like Chaucer and Clanvowe, were becoming literate, and in their education taking over the set of ideas formerly and more naturally held by churchmen, and especially by monks. This development is seen at its beginning in the writing of Henry of Lancaster, but the contrast between 'thisworldliness' and 'other-worldliness' was not yet very sharp. It rapidly became sharper with the next generation, which included Chaucer and his friends. There seems to be a major inconsistency between their opinions and their lives.

To take Clanvowe's life as an example, we should hardly guess from it the nature of the opinions, commonplace as they were for clerics, that are expressed in his treatise. Clanvowe was a distinguished soldier and diplomat of about the same age as Chaucer. He was a Herefordshire man, and prominent in the affairs of his county, but he was a member of Joan of Kent's inner circle, like Clifford, Stury, and Latimer, and was a close friend of William Neville. All these were accused by chroniclers of being Lollards, and they were also associates of Chaucer's. Clanvowe was one of the leaders of a successful diplomatic mission to France in 1389 to negotiate a truce. In the following year he went on a crusade to Barbary, in which Clifford and Neville also took part. According to the author of the *Polychronicon*, he died on 17th October 1391 while on a journey to Constantinople with his inseparable friend Neville. It was said that Neville would not take food for grief at the death of his friend, and himself died two days after.

It is surprising to find Clanvowe and his friends on crusades, however military, for the Lollards condemned crusades. It is this kind of inconsistency that has led some scholars to deny the importance of Lollardy in courtly circles; but that goes too far. The chroniclers Walsingham and Knighton accused some ten knights of Lollardy, and there is no doubt that at least some of these were Lollards for a long time. One of the most outstanding was Chaucer's and Deschamps' friend, Sir Lewis Clifford, and there is no doubt that he did not recant until 1402. Latimer, another of them, undoubtedly owned and lent out Lollard books; Sir John Montague, eventually third Earl of Salisbury, harboured Lollard priests and destroyed images; Stury recanted; Clanvowe wrote the treatise that has already been quoted from, and so on. Furthermore, these men and some others are so closely associated in a number of records that they can only be regarded as a group of more or less like-minded friends. And it would be easy to add the names of others who were clearly associated with them, by marriage, as executors of each other's wills, and in other such ways. What is particularly interesting is that Chaucer is one of those who, while not being quite of the inner circle, was close to it, through his association with various individuals in it. They were all men of affairs. For the most part they had had distinguished military careers, and then were occupied in either Richard's or his mother's household, as courtiers, politicians, and administrators, like Chaucer himself. Like Chaucer, too, they had a taste both for polite literature and for serious writings on religion, philosophy and science. They were in fact very much in the forefront of their age in all respects, not least in religion. Chaucer himself makes a mild joke in *The Canterbury Tales* which probably refers in some way to his Lollard friends. The Parson objects to the Host's swearing, at which the Host sneers 'I smell a Loller in the wind', and goes on to say that now we can expect a fine sermon. This prospect horrifies the Shipman. There is no reason to suppose, however, that the Parson is actually meant to be thought a Lollard.

But this passage was probably written about 1389-90 (though

that is only a guess) and in 1389, according to Walsingham, there had been a great fuss about Lollards in London, especially about pilgrimages, which the Lollards condemned, and the subject was clearly in the air. The difficulty is to say exactly what *was* Lollardy, especially as it concerned those inconsistent gentlemen, the so-called Lollard knights.

In some respects Lollardy was simply the expression of laymen taking more seriously the normal doctrines of the medieval Church as they became better educated. Clanvowe's treatise is an example of this. Apart from his reference to 'lollers', a name he obviously takes to himself, there is nothing very unusual in his treatise except possibly the frequent reference to the Bible. What makes it remarkable is that it was written by a knight, who was living the life he was consciously condemning. Chaucer shows the same tendency. He was a layman, but highly educated, which in itself was unusual, compared with the earlier part of the century, and he spent many hours in the laborious translation of the long sermon which is *The Parson's Tale*. He drew the beautiful portrait of the ideal Parson in the *General Prologue*; there are no specific Lollard doctrines in that portrait, which in some ways reflects the constant Christian ideal of the priest throughout the ages, but it is one which comes very close to what may be gathered of Lollard ideals. Chaucer also wrote a lot of religious poetry, and he wrote a religious ending to *Troilus and Criseyde* which has puzzled many rationalist critics. And at the end of his life he actually condemned his non-religious writings. All this suggests that at the end of the century there was a spirit of lay devotion among courtiers and others which, whatever their sinful lives, showed a growth of sincere thought about religious truth. Naturally, it grew out of the normal moral teaching, and showed itself in some ways as a kind of medieval puritanism.

Equally naturally, this new thought and deeper feeling led men to question some of the accepted truths, and since they were not trained thinkers, some of their questioning was crudely simple. The doctrine of images, for example, seemed to them to be pure idolatry, as it undoubtedly was among many simple souls. So Montague destroyed the images on his estate. They were conscious of great abuses in the Church, and the great misuse of the Church's wealth, and this led some to propose that the Church's wealth should be taken away, being also encouraged, no doubt, by the less spiritual thought that they might themselves make good personal use of such wealth. The difficult doctrine of the Real Presence of God in the consecration of the bread and wine of the Mass seemed to them absurd, like image-worship, and Walsingham called the Lollard knights the 'hooded' knights, because they refused to take off their hats before the consecrated bread and wine. Paradoxically, both the sceptical irreligion mentioned earlier, and the serious care for more rational religion of at least some Lollards, could lead to much the same attitude to the corrupt and over-ceremonious medieval church. Both scepticism and the desire for more rational, more spiritual religion might have the same root, might even co-exist in the same man.

In most of this it is plain, as later events showed, that the knights only reflected the feelings and thoughts of great numbers of English people. The Londoners were particularly affected by the new movement, and the bitterly hostile monk Walsingham says that vast numbers of people were of the same opinions throughout the country. It is, in fact, the first stirrings of what came to a head in the sixteenth century as the Reformation. And just as in the sixteenth century, so in the fourteenth century, the movement was remarkable for the demand to read the Bible. Chaucer's knowledge of the Bible is very considerable, but he could read Latin. Others could not, and there was a great desire to have the Bible in English, as is shown by the number of copies that have survived from the fifteenth century.

This, however, introduces a complication, the effect of Wycliffe's work, about which there is still debate. A quarrelsome and stiff-necked Yorkshireman, he was born about 1320, and went to Balliol College. He remained at Oxford most of his life, lecturing in the schools, writing vast works, and distinguished rather for the force and energy of his mind than for great originality. We see the natural inconsistency of the age in his attacks on such abuses as absentee priests when we find that he drew most of his income for most of his life from parishes from which he was himself absent. He first got into intellectual difficulties in his treatment of the doctrine of the Real Presence. In this he was like many a scholar and theologian before him; the schools were naturally, one may say properly, a hot-bed of heresy, since they were devoted to passionate disputation and inquiry. What made Wycliffe different was his refusal to recant when he was proclaimed in error. He also developed the doctrine that all authority is founded on grace; so that those who were considered to be without grace could be refused authority. At one time this doctrine seemed useful in the longlasting political disagreements of the English Crown with the Pope, and he was given some diplomatic employment, of the kind often given to highly trained university men. He attacked the usual abuses, and for a time his anti-clericalism also made him seem useful to John of Gaunt. Wycliffe was no diplomat, however. His teachings became more and more extreme. After the Pope had condemned his doctrine of grace he moved on to attack the Pope, and when, at the Great Schism, which began in 1377, the two Popes both claimed the usual papal authority (and taxes), he declared the Papacy to be Antichrist itself. He condemned the whole structure of the medieval Church, denied the Real Presence, and considered that the whole wealth of the Church should be taken away. He also taught that every man should be enabled to read the Bible for himself. It is easy to see how he offended everyone in authority, both clerical and lay. Some people laid the responsibility for the Peasants' Revolt at his door, though this was certainly mistaken. But the Revolt almost certainly increased the anxiety and seriousness with which his teachings were regarded by authority, and he was condemned, as has been mentioned, in 1382, at the Synod of Blackfriars. He retired to his parsonage at Lutterworth, and died in 1384.

Although he offended so many, it is also easy to see that he gave intellectual expression to ideas and feelings that were very widespread. Perhaps this is the reason why he himself was condemned, but not persecuted. It is true that the English bishops were not used to heresy, from which England had been notably free. In addition, the English as a whole had a commendable reluctance to use the violent forms of persecution, and to employ torture and burning. But there was a sense in which Wycliffe expressed what many people felt, and the bishops themselves, when not too busy administering the kingdom, may have responded to this. Archbishop Sudbury's toleration of Lollardy was notable, but Walsingham gets furious with all the other bishops, except Despenser of Norwich, for also tolerating Lollardy. The intolerant and intolerable Despenser (he who organised the scandalous crusade against the Flemings) threatened to kill any Lollards he found in his diocese, much to Walsingham's delight. For of course the opposition to Wycliffe and the ideas associated with him was very strong, even among those not in authority. He took things rather too far. Even in Oxford, where his following was greatest, the energetic Archbishop Courtenay, who had succeeded Sudbury, and who organised the synod at Blackfriars, was able to crush Wycliffism, when he descended like a wolf on the fold just after the synod, and made Wycliffe's most prominent disciples recant. This crushing of the intellectual life of Oxford was most successful, and reflected on the whole intellectual life of the kingdom throughout the fifteenth century. English religion became notable for its piety, but 'Reason was under'. When Bishop Pekok, in the middle of the fifteenth century, appealed to reason as well as

Archbishop Courtenay, Canterbury

to authority in his attacks on Lollardy, he had his books burned by the very authority he was trying to defend.

Lollardy may be said to have taken over Wycliffe's ideas, rather than to have been brought into being by them. After his death the programme continued to develop. Copies of the English translation of the Bible, which he had inspired, multiplied. Poor men met and discussed religion; poor preachers travelled about. In London the movement had a more political and deliberately anti-clerical side, with elaborate manifestos pinned up on the doors of St Paul's. Some of the upper-class adherents were slow to drop away; Sir

Lewis Clifford did not recant until 1402. A host of tracts and sermons in English were written and widely distributed, advocating something like the later Reformation doctrine of the priesthood of all believers, condemning image-worship, ceremonies (including that of marriage), pilgrimages, crusades, war, and the observance of Sunday. More and more evidence has come to light suggesting that Lollardy did not die in the fifteenth century. It led to an abortive revolt under Sir John Oldcastle in 1414. Some brave men were burnt. But for the most part, continually attacked, it went underground throughout the century, until it blazed out again in the Reformation. Wycliffe's own writings in Latin seem to have had little influence in England. They deeply influenced Huss in Bohemia, who in his turn is said to have influenced Luther, whose writings exercised their influence on England in the sixteenth century. Wycliffe's intellectual influence thus may be said to have rejoined again the feelings it had first met in the fourteenth century.

Nevertheless, Wycliffe's condemnation, and the energetic measures that followed it, took the intellectual stuffing out of Lollardy in England. All the strivings and sufferings of uneducated or half-educated folk could not supply the force of mind, and religion, like literature, was enfeebled throughout the fifteenth century by its lack. Nor could the courtiers supply what was wanted. Even the vein of intellectual scepticism, noticeable in Chaucer, and bitterly commented on by Langland, that was a minor characteristic of the upper classes in the later fourteenth century, and which also probably derived from Oxford, seems to be lacking in the fifteenth century. The passing stirring of the heart and mind, of which Lollardy was only a more extreme example in the later fourteenth century, left the outer body and dress of organised religion pretty well as they were, except for the growth among the orthodox of an occasionally more feverish and morbid piety. And such a result was emotionally, socially, artistically, and spiritually satisfying to many good and orthodox people.

There is no doubt, either, that the body of orthodox Christian practice and doctrine as it was then understood also satisfied that myriad-minded man Geoffrey Chaucer, for all his sympathy with the new spirit of devotion. His work reveals the same mixture of the devout and the worldly that one sees in the life of his times. Even in the lightest flippancy, even at his most sceptical, even in *fabliaux* like the *Miller's*, *Reeve's* and *Shipman's Tales*, there is a firm underlying moral structure which takes its strength from the religious and ethical ideals of his times, and which shows the power of those ideals in moulding thought and feeling. Although Chaucer's writing is not realistic in the way that we have become used to, there is no doubt that it penetrates and is penetrated by life, to an extent that more realistic writing often fails to achieve. And since, for all its interest in death, forced on it by circumstances, medieval Christianity was primarily a way of life that with all its failures moulded the whole English people, we must grant its value and power in Chaucer's work. Chaucer's life, also, reflects the mixture of the worldly and devout. Whatever his sins, whatever his struggles for his own advantage, however mocking he may have been at times, when age came on him he took a little house in the precincts of Westminster Abbey, as many another man took up final refuge under the shelter of a monastery. It is not surprising that he condemned all his secular works, in the epilogue or recantation that he added to the end of *The Canterbury Tales*. Both his writing of such tales, and his final condemnation of them, were fully in accord with the spirit of his time. Like the cleverest people in all ages, he managed to eat his cake and have it too.

Nor need we suppose him obsessed with the gloomier fears of death. Bishop Brinton says that only a bad man need fear death. Theseus in *The Knight's Tale*, in the noble speech with which the poem is concluded, declares that all is sent from 'Jupiter', and all must return to him. Let us after woe make merry. Troilus, when killed and carried up into the heavenly spheres, looks down upon this little spot of earth

And in hymself he lough right at the wo   *laughed*
Of hem that wepten for his deth so faste;
And dampned al oure werk that foloweth so
The blynde lust, the which that may nat laste,   *pleasure*
And sholden al oure herte on heven caste.

If there is something very sharp and surprising in the laughter, coming after so much worldly sorrow and joy, there is nothing in it out of accord with the spirit of medieval Christianity and of Chaucer himself.

INDEX